Praise for
Nine Thoughts That Can Change Your Marriage

"In my research with happy marriages ~~...~~ ppy wives
have one thing in comm~~...~~ esn't just
happen. Sheila gives ~~...~~ entional
thinking about what go~~...~~ nails it!
Here's to a new generatio~~...~~

— FAWN WEAVER, *~~...~~ imes* best-selling author of
Happy Wives Club

"What a wonderful book! The teaching points are inspiring, and the action steps truly can be marriage-transforming. Many readers will particularly appreciate Sheila's delightful way of challenging conventional wisdom as she offers freshly applied biblical wisdom. One of the best things you could do for your spouse, your children, and your own happiness and contentment in the coming year is to read and apply *Nine Thoughts That Can Change Your Marriage*."

— GARY THOMAS, author of *Sacred Marriage*

"The truths in *Nine Thoughts That Can Change Your Marriage* hold the power to revolutionize relationships. Sheila Wray Gregoire gives it to us straight: we *can* be happy, we *can* have the good marriage that God designed. But first we need to change our thought life. As Sheila challenges pat answers and common misconceptions about what makes a marriage work, she offers an alternate, hope-filled path. Her real-life examples and biblical insights will free you to approach your marriage with a transformed attitude and renewed energy."

— SHANNON ETHRIDGE, relationship coach, speaker, and author of the bestseller *Every Woman's Battle*

"In this lively and engaging book, Sheila doesn't just explode cultural myths about marriage and replace them with biblical truth; she also provides ultrapractical tasks for wives to apply their new knowledge. I love the emphasis on working on yourself *first,* rather than trying to change your spouse."

—SHAUNTI FELDHAHN, social researcher and best-selling
   author of *For Women Only*

"We've all heard the adage, 'It takes two to make a marriage work.' And it's true. But with *Nine Thoughts That Can Change Your Marriage,* Sheila Wray Gregoire gives women powerful tools to make a huge difference in their marriages all on their own. Instead of focusing on what our husbands should do, Sheila helps us focus on what we as wives actually can do. Actionable, empowering, and freeing."

—KATHI LIPP, author of *The Husband Project*

"Sheila takes us on a journey of discovering how our personal thoughts may be interfering with our marriage and gives us practical steps on how to make the lasting change we long for and desperately need!"

—RUTH SCHWENK, speaker, author, and creator
   of TheBetterMom.com

"Sheila wisely helps women think healthy thoughts so they can create a healthier marriage. Think honest, loving, practical, biblical, relevant—those are the kind of wise thoughts Sheila will help you think so you can discover the power to build a love to look forward to living."

—PAM FARREL, best-selling author of *Red Hot Monogamy*

"In *Nine Thoughts That Can Change Your Marriage,* Sheila Wray Gregoire challenges spouses to take the focus off of what their marriage partner is doing 'wrong' and, instead, change their own thought patterns to see their spouse in a whole new light. She is transparent about how her own faulty thinking created struggles early in her marriage, and she celebrates how God redeemed her situation to create the beautiful relationship she now enjoys with her husband."

—ERIN ODOM, creator of TheHumbledHomemaker.com

9 Thoughts
That Can Change
Your Marriage

9 Thoughts
That Can Change
Your Marriage

Because a Great Relationship
Doesn't Happen by Accident

SHEILA WRAY GREGOIRE

WATERBROOK
PRESS

NINE THOUGHTS THAT CAN CHANGE YOUR MARRIAGE
PUBLISHED BY WATERBROOK PRESS
12265 Oracle Boulevard, Suite 200
Colorado Springs, Colorado 80921

This book is not intended to replace the advice of a trained psychological professional. Readers are advised to consult a qualified professional regarding treatment of their psychological and emotional problems. The author and publisher specifically disclaim liability, loss, or risk, personal or otherwise, which is incurred as a consequence, directly or indirectly, of the use or application of any of the contents of this book.

All Scripture quotations, unless otherwise indicated, are taken from the Holy Bible, New International Version®, NIV®. Copyright © 1973, 1978, 1984, 2011 by Biblica Inc.™ Used by permission of Zondervan. All rights reserved worldwide. www.zondervan.com. Scripture quotations marked (KJV) are taken from the King James Version. Scripture quotations marked (NLT) are taken from the Holy Bible, New Living Translation, copyright © 1996, 2004, 2007. Used by permission of Tyndale House Publishers Inc., Carol Stream, Illinois 60188. All rights reserved. Scripture quotations marked (NRSV) are from the New Revised Standard Version of the Bible, copyright © 1989 by the Division of Christian Education of the National Council of the Churches of Christ in the USA. Used by permission. All rights reserved.

Italics in Scripture quotations reflect the author's added emphasis.

Details in some anecdotes and stories have been changed to protect the identities of the persons involved.

Trade Paperback ISBN 978-1-60142-708-3
eBook ISBN 978-1-60142-709-0

Cover design by Kelly L. Howard; cover photography by Eric O'Connell

Published in the United States by WaterBrook Multnomah, an imprint of the Crown Publishing Group, a division of Penguin Random House LLC, New York.

WATERBROOK and its deer colophon are registered trademarks of Penguin Random House LLC.

The Cataloging-in-Publication Data is on file with the Library of Congress.

Printed in the United States of America
2015—First Edition

10 9 8 7 6 5 4 3 2 1

SPECIAL SALES
Most WaterBrook Multnomah books are available at special quantity discounts when purchased in bulk by corporations, organizations, and special-interest groups. Custom imprinting or excerpting can also be done to fit special needs. For information, please e-mail SpecialMarkets@WaterBrookMultnomah.com or call 1-800-603-7051.

To Rebecca and Connor:
With prayers for a long and blessed life together.
July 18, 2015

Contents

Thought #7

Thought #8

Thought #9

We Do What We Think!

My husband, Keith, and I have been married twenty-three years and happily married for eighteen. Those first five years were awful. Sex was awful. School was awful. Our social life was awful. We talked past each other rather than with each other.

Yet we managed to leave marital misery behind and emerge, only slightly scathed, to marital bliss. I'm firmly convinced it's because we are both extremely stubborn. Neither of us was willing to allow our marriage to fail. But perhaps even more important, both of us are extremely loud. When we were mad, we talked about it. We cried about it. At times, I'm ashamed to admit, we even yelled about it. And slowly but surely we experienced some breakthroughs—and the house grew a lot quieter.

I'm not sure, though, that I did any of these things the "right" way, at least if you measure "right" by how a Nice Christian Girl is supposed to act. You likely know that girl. She's demure, yet she's strong as a tiger. She submits enthusiastically, yet she has a mind of her own. She never speaks up or criticizes her husband, yet she is insightful and cunning enough to "win him without words."[1] Her house is organized, her children make crafts, and her husband is proud as a peacock.

I am not that girl. If I have an opinion, I'm incapable of keeping it to myself. I am only industrious in bursts, when I finally lose it and become the very model of a modern wifely drill sergeant. I have fed my children chocolate cake for breakfast, although I did so only because they saw me eating it first and it seemed fair. I don't always dust. I go to McDonald's too often. And I don't order the salads.

I may be a miserable failure as far as the Perfect Christian Wife is concerned, yet I have a good, solid marriage. My husband and I feel as if we are one.

That feeling, however, was not automatic. And for me, the problem started in the bedroom.

Keith and I had both waited for marriage to have sex, and we both assumed that it would be wonderful, mind-blowing, and perfectly natural. But it wasn't. It was awkward, it was messy, and worst of all, it hurt. Whenever Keith wanted to make love, I felt rejected, because he wanted something that made me miserable. My frustration finally grew to the point where I wondered, *Why can't he just love me for me and not for what I can do for him?* I accused him of selfishness. Of not loving me. Of being a Neanderthal who couldn't control his passions. The more we fought over sex, the more certain I became that he didn't value me. I felt so lonely, and yet instead of being sympathetic and wrapping me in a bear hug, Keith lobbed accusations right back: "Why don't you care about my feelings? Why don't you want me?"

After I had prayed for two exhausting years that he would start caring about me, a thought entered my head: *Do you believe the only one who can fix this relationship is Keith? Don't you have something to do with it?* I didn't particularly like that thought, and so I vehemently argued with myself about why changing was impossible. Even if we only considered sex, how was I supposed to enjoy something so gross and uncomfortable?

Then another thought hit me even harder: *If God says that sex is good, and the whole world says that sex is good, maybe you should start figuring out how to make sex good.*

I was stunned. If that thought was right, then the responsibility fell on me to do something about my struggle. I had to stop thinking sex was awful and start thinking, *Sex is great—I just don't have it all figured out yet.* The problem may have started in the bedroom, but it wasn't a problem with sex. It was a problem with how I was thinking.

The next few years in our marriage became my big research project into this thing called *Us.* I decided to conquer this sex issue once and for all, because if God created something this great, no way was I going to miss it! I read books and talked to friends about how to make sex work. I talked to wise mentors about how to deal with past issues that held people back. I studied Keith to glean what made him feel loved. Slowly but surely, I fell madly in love with Keith again. And thankfully, he with me too.

FAULTY THINKING LEAVES US STUCK

My marriage was stuck when I believed that Keith's libido was the cause of all our fights. After all, if his sex drive was the problem, then the only solution I could see was to make Keith want sex less. I threw my energy into that dead-end goal: I bought a wardrobe of long flannel nightgowns; I complained constantly about headaches; and I stopped kissing in all its forms.

I was fruitlessly expending all this energy, making myself and my husband frustrated, because I suffered from faulty thinking. It was only when I realized that I had a different option—instead of investing so much energy into getting Keith to want sex less, I could figure out how to make me want it more—did things begin to change.

When our options are limited, it's easy to become hopeless. I believed that my marriage couldn't get better until Keith changed, but I had no control over that. So I was stuck. And when you're stuck, you stop trying—or you do counterproductive things, such as emptying out the local Salvation Army of all their granny nightgowns. You're not fixing your marriage; you're digging a deeper hole.

But what if that initial thought was wrong? What if peace and joy are not dependent on someone else changing, but they instead flow from God giving us the ability to choose how to think, how to feel, and how to respond? We can choose to make our life fulfilling by aligning our thoughts more with God's. Jesus, after all, isn't just our way to salvation. He is Truth itself (John 14:6). When we grow close to Jesus, he reveals Truth. That lets us see all the options before us. Then we won't feel stuck—we'll know that there is always a way forward.

CHRISTIANS GET STUCK TOO

That sounds a bit like a clichéd bumper sticker, though, doesn't it? "Are you stuck? You just need Jesus!" While this pat statement has a foundation of truth, if it were really that easy, wouldn't all Christians have great marriages?

Yes, we would, and I think it's to our shame that we don't. But I've seen lots of faulty thinking in Christian circles that goes something like this:

> If you have a problem in your marriage, then the answer is always to pray more, submit more, or love more. If you just pray more, your husband will stop the porn. If you just submit more, your husband will become a leader and stop playing all those video games. If you just love him more, he'll stop being a workaholic and start remembering your birthday. Do these things, and your husband will change and you will be happy.

Now prayer, of course, is one of the best weapons we have in bringing peace to our lives, and I certainly don't mean to discount its importance. But the reason *behind* the prayer matters. If you pray only to get God to do something, then you treat God like Santa Claus or a rabbit's foot, not a Savior with a claim on your life. Prayer should always be about submission to God's will; it should not be about convincing God to do yours. Similarly, submission and love are among the noblest pursuits, but if your purpose in doing them is to cajole your husband into changing to make you happy, then that's manipulation too. And your faulty thinking—that you need your husband to change in order for you to be happy—limits your options for improving your marriage. You're stuck.

These ideas that enter our consciousness—that by praying and loving enough we will have a happy marriage—are what I will call "pat answers." They promise the moon and make marriage look so easy. But despite the initial seduction of the "promise," ultimately these pat answers don't work, because they put the responsibility for change in someone else's hands. It's not you, fully submitted to God, who acts to bring about change; it's God all by himself, or your husband, or a friend. You become a bystander.

In this book we'll look at nine thoughts that will change the way you look at your marriage and show you the options you have for making it awesome.

But the very first choice we need to make is the most basic. It's one I figured out twenty years ago, and one that I pray we'll all realize: God made us responsible for our own actions, our own thoughts, and our own feelings. No one else can do that work for us.

Does that sound heavy, as though God will blame you if things go wrong? It does a little, doesn't it? But I actually think having responsibility is freeing.

God is an active God. He created the universe with a word (Genesis 1). He intervenes in human affairs to bring glory to his name, to bring justice to the earth, and to care for those he loves.

And he created us to act as well—that's what it means when people say we have "free will." We have the ability to choose. We don't have to be bystanders.

Living a godly life means acting and doing in God's power; it doesn't mean sitting back and waiting for someone else to act. Too often this is what women have been counseled to do. It has meant that women have put up with too much. But it has also meant that we haven't been "strong in the Lord"[2]; we haven't fought using God's power to bring about God's will on earth as it is in heaven. We've been stuck, waiting for someone else to change. And our marriages, and by extension our families and communities, have suffered for it.

HOW TO USE THIS BOOK

In the rest of the book, I share with you nine thoughts, all with their own action steps, that will lead to real change in our marriages. The first four thoughts have to do with confronting our own hearts and attitudes and are probably the most difficult to read. It's so much easier to point to other people as the cause of our unhappiness, but I encourage you to look first at what is in your control—and then do something about it.

Thoughts five through seven have to do with our roles in marriage, especially when it comes to dealing with conflicts. When we need to resolve big issues, how do we do it biblically, as husband and wife?

Finally, we'll turn from big-picture issues about attitude and conflict and look at the day-to-day tensions in married life. We'll see how failure to give our sexual life and our emotional life the right energy can end up stealing our joy with our husbands.

It's that joy that I want for you. I know what it is to have a happy marriage, and I know what it is to have a lonely marriage. The difference between the two, for me, was largely about attitude. I just needed to change perspective. I hope that in this book I can help you see your husband, and your marriage too, through a different lens.

I don't know what kind of marriage you have. Maybe you're usually happy but sometimes your husband drives you completely batty. Maybe you feel alone most of the time. Maybe you and your husband have become comfortable roommates, and you wonder where the passion has gone.

Most of us go through periods in marriage when we're closer and periods when we're more distant. I think that's why marriage is a decades-long relationship—it gives us a chance to weather those storms and find each other again!

Wherever you are in your marriage, whether you're in the middle of a close period or trudging through a rough patch, I pray this book will give you some new perspectives on your relationship that can jump-start the change you yearn for.

Thought #1

My Husband Is My Neighbor

My husband grew up the oldest of four boys, with a stay-at-home mom and a blue-collar dad. My father walked out when I was two, leaving me the only child of a single mother who worked in a high-powered public-sector job. Keith's house was loud, with frequent wrestling matches and fistfights, some involving billiard balls. My house was quiet; I used to play chess against myself—and often lost.

When Keith was young, he had season tickets to the local junior league hockey team. I had season tickets to the National Ballet of Canada.

He lived in a small town. I lived in downtown Toronto.

At the age of six I began flying by myself to see my dad, and by age eighteen I had traveled to Europe alone. Keith didn't board a plane until he was nineteen.

My favorite food was sushi. Keith's perfect meal was roast beef, mashed potatoes, and canned peas.

And yet he was my one true love. We met in university, where we quickly became best friends. After my teenage years, during which I made a complete idiot of myself trying to get friends to adore me, I finally met someone who accepted me just as I was. We laughed together. We led a youth group together. We were kindred spirits. I was certain that he would be the one who would make me happy for the rest of my life.

Then we walked down the aisle, and suddenly this man who had understood me and completed me and loved me had actual expectations and demands—expectations that clashed with my reality.

As I mentioned earlier, most of our problems were with sex. The more Keith wanted it, the more I felt he only loved me for what I could do for him. So I would pray, "God, please help him see how much he's hurting me. Help him just to love me again." I'd pour out my heart, certain that the God who wipes away tears would hear me and answer me. But sometimes that truth—that "the LORD is close to the brokenhearted and saves those who are crushed in spirit" (Psalm 34:18)—morphs into something more like this:

> **Pat Answer:** *God is close to the brokenhearted. So cast your cares onto him! Draw close to him, because your pain matters, and he wants to do battle on your behalf so that those who are breaking your heart will stop.*

If God is close to the brokenhearted, then he must want to avenge those who are brokenhearted, right?

I did everything the pat answer told me to do: I prayed. I cast my cares on God. I drew close to him. Yet my prayers didn't work.

Keith still got grumpy when I would respond negatively to his friskiness. He still didn't understand how I felt. And I was still lonely.

I wanted a marriage where my husband understood and cherished and valued me. Didn't I deserve that? So what was Keith's problem? And more to the point, what was God's problem? I was doing my part, after all.

Slowly but surely, God gave me that marriage—just not in the way I expected. God didn't heal my broken heart by going to battle with Keith for me; God healed my broken heart by helping me see that Keith was hurting too, and that by my reaching out to him—and figuring out this sex thing—I could bridge that gulf. God didn't want to zap Keith and rescue me; God wanted me to stop hanging back and focusing on my hurts and instead devote some of that energy toward Keith.

I wish I could say that I mastered this twenty years ago, after our early tensions, but I still need the occasional reminder. Just recently, Keith and I were smack in the middle of one of those busy seasons where all our energy was channeled at keeping all the plates in the air from crashing down, and we didn't have much left for each other. Keith had a huge block of time scheduled at the hospital (he's a pediatrician), and extroverted me, who never handles solitude well, became a bit of a bear.

While Keith was away on call, I began chewing on an old hurt. I had suffered many rejections as a child and teenager, but when I met my husband, I thought that finally I had a man who would love me completely just for being me. So I was shocked when cold feet caused him to call off our initial engagement.

Thankfully the estrangement wasn't long, but that rejection pierced me. When I walked through a season recently when it seemed as if fellow committee members and church friends and blog readers were all disappointed in me, those feelings of rejection came flooding back. And with it came the reminder of my husband's rejection from long ago.

When Keith's long bout of hospital calls was over, I finally had an audience with whom to vent these feelings. But it's rarely a good idea to stay up talking about deep issues when you're tired; you just blow things out of proportion. And I didn't simply blow them up. I stuck them in a cannon, fired at Keith's weakest points, and came pretty close to cheering when I hit the mark.

Then Keith said something really important: "I just need to know that *us* matters more than *you*." He wasn't saying that my feelings didn't matter; he wasn't even saying that his feelings mattered more than mine. He was reminding me that we are on the same side, and that I should fight for that unity, even when my feelings were hurt.

My husband is a very smart man. He knew that we would never feel unity if we were always nursing our own hurts.

I think that is God's heart for us too. He's not on my side; he's on his own side—and his desire for my husband and me is to be "one flesh."[1] When we fixate on our own broken hearts and believe that God's main desire is to take those hurts away, then we're not treating God as the Master of the Universe. We're treating him like our own personal genie, ready to do our bidding.

In his book *Accidental Pharisees,* author Larry Osborne explains how we can make God a little too personal:

Most of us tend to read every *you* in the Bible as if it were a first-person singular pronoun, even though most are plurals (the Southern *y'all*). We treat every promise and command as if it were ours, aimed directly at us and our circumstances. . . .

On one level, that can be a good thing, if it causes us to treat our Bibles as a life manual. But on another level, it can be a bad thing, especially when it fosters a skewed, "I'm at the center of God's universe" spirituality.[2]

Yes, God is close to the brokenhearted—but he is close to *all* the brokenhearted, not just us. God cares about our husbands' hearts too.

How Does God Feel
When We're at Odds with Each Other?

The hardest period of parenting for me was when my girls were between the ages of nine and twelve. One had hit puberty and the other hadn't yet. These two lovely girls, who used to play together and giggle together, suddenly were yelling at each other and tattling on each other and making each other cry. Whenever Katie drew a picture of Rebecca, she stuck devil horns on her. Whenever Katie went into Rebecca's room, Rebecca would kick her out. As a mom, it broke my heart.

I repeated it like a mantra, "She is your best friend, even if you don't feel it. She's the one who will still be in your life when you're sixty. You had better start being nicer to her now."

Time and maturity healed their rift, and we all laugh now at Katie's notebook filled with devil horns and Rebecca's diary filled with vitriolic scrawlings. But at the time it wasn't funny. It hurt me deeply to see my two precious children so quick to wound each other.

When there's tension in our marriages, I wonder if God hurts like that too. You and your husband are both his children, and yet there you are, often at odds with each other.

Gary Thomas, the author of *Sacred Marriage,* put it this way: Would your perspective about your husband change if you realized not just that God was your Father, but that God was also your Father-in-law?[3] He isn't just the Daddy who holds you close and assures you of his love when you're feeling down. He's also the Daddy who wants to comfort your husband. God wants the best for you—*but he also wants the best for your mate.*

He wants for your husband the same thing he wants for you: to have a spouse who is a best friend, a great lover, and a cheerleader to encourage and build him up when he starts to doubt himself. He wants your husband to have someone who will help him cling to God, someone who will spur him on to even greater deeds and to great influence in this life.

And for all of that, God chose you.

Yes, God also chose your husband for you, and yes, he also wants your husband to fulfill those things in your life. But God looked at you and thought, *Here is a woman for my son.*

Think about that. God has trusted you with this precious son of his. *And he wants your husband to feel loved.*

What Does Loving My Husband Look Like?

A long time ago, a rich man asked Jesus how he could be a good enough person to get eternal life. Jesus turned the question back on him and asked him what the Scriptures said. This rich, smart young man summarized all the Scriptures with two basic commandments: "'Love the Lord your God with all your heart and with all your soul and with all your strength and with all your mind'; and 'Love your neighbor as yourself'" (Luke 10:27). Jesus thought this was a good answer and told him so.

But this left the man in a bit of a quandary. Loving your neighbor as yourself is a pretty big task, because, if this rich guy was anything like me, I love myself quite a lot. So if I'm supposed to treat my neighbor the way I want to be treated, that's a lot of nice pills I'm going to have to swallow.

The man wanted some clarification, or at least a bit of wiggle room, so he asked Jesus, "Who is my neighbor?" (verse 29).

That's when Jesus told him a story about a Samaritan—a person from a despised racial and religious group—who saw a naked, beaten-up guy lying on the side of the road. The Samaritan picked him up, dressed his wounds, and took him to safety, paying for him to be cared for.

What's remarkable about this action, though, is that other people who were closer in kinship to the beaten-up guy walked by before the Samaritan arrived and did absolutely nothing. A priest and a Levite, who were supposed to be generous toward someone in need, chose to ignore the guy's desperate plight. It took a stranger to offer aid.

After telling this story, Jesus asked, "Who acted like the guy's neighbor?"

"The one who helped him," the rich man replied.

And Jesus told him to go and act like a neighbor.

The lesson we often take from that parable is that God wants us to love everybody, near and far. But if he wants us to love everybody, then that automatically includes our husbands.

Thought #1:
My husband is
my neighbor.

Our husbands are our neighbors, and so God wants us to love our husbands as well as we love ourselves.

That doesn't mean we don't love ourselves, or that our needs and feelings don't matter to God; he simply wants us to care as deeply for the man we married.

But is that easier said than done? Another thing this story shows us is that the one who helped the Samaritan was not a priest or a Levite (who would be expected to help). It was someone much further removed. I don't think that's all that surprising, because it's often easier to feel compassion for people in the abstract than for individuals we know up close and personal. We know our loved ones' flaws, so it's easier to justify not coming to the rescue.

Sure, your husband may be stressed, but it's his fault because he spends way too much time on video games and not enough time brushing up on his work skills that could help him avoid the next round of layoffs. Sure, he may be upset because you don't make love enough, but if he just put in some effort to make your life simpler, then perhaps it would be easier for you to also put in some effort. You can see how he has contributed to the problem.

When we see a stranger in pain, though, we don't know the backstory, so we simply see that person as *human*. Our husbands, on the other hand, we often classify as either deserving or undeserving. And it's all too easy to dismiss their needs simply because we know too much.

Action Step: How well do you know your husband? Every day for the next two weeks, ask your husband to tell you something you don't know about him—and volunteer something new about yourself. Who was his first crush? What did he want to grow up to be when he was seven? Whose was the first funeral he went to? Search "conversation starters" on the Internet for more ideas. Get to know your husband better than you know anybody else.

TREATING OUR HUSBANDS AS WELL AS WE TREAT OUR NEIGHBORS

I have this sneaking suspicion that most of us save our best behavior for those whom we barely know and show our worst side to those we know the best. Here's just a minor example: I'm a makeup kind of gal. Lipstick makes me happy, and when you combine it with lip gloss I'm ecstatic. And I really don't like other people seeing me *au naturel*. If I'm heading out to the grocery store, I put on makeup first. I'll stick gel in my hair. It may only take three minutes, but I try to pretty myself up. If I'm heading out to dinner with friends, I change clothes and put on a nice blouse so I look special.

One day it occurred to me, *I am putting in all this effort so that strangers think I'm pretty, and yet my husband, who is really the only one who is supposed to admire me, gets little effort from me on his own.* I was doing everything backward! So now fifteen minutes before Keith walks in the door, I head upstairs and put on a little lipstick and mascara, and I style my hair. I want him to know that he is the one who is most special to me, and he deserves my best, not my leftovers.

Your husband is your neighbor. Your husband deserves to have you love him as you love yourself. And that means it should matter to you if he feels unloved, even if you feel unloved too.

Does that mean he gets away scot-free with treating you badly? No, it doesn't, and later in this book we'll talk at length about how to solve big problems—and some not so big, but awfully annoying ones. I am not saying that conflict should be swept under the rug. I am simply pointing out that God loves your husband and wants you to love him too.

Action Step: Find one practical way to show your husband that he—not a stranger—is your priority. Here are some ideas: put on makeup and fix your appearance before you meet up at the end of the day; stand up to greet him when he gets home— or kiss him first when you do; or always get him his favorite drink when you get up to get yours. Pick one and make it a daily habit!

LOVING MY MAN SHOULDN'T BE ROCKET SCIENCE

Here's the good news: I have this inkling that it's easier for us to figure out how to make our husbands feel loved than it is for them to figure out how to make us feel loved.

About a year or so ago, my husband and I walked through another of our busy seasons. (Unfortunately, these seem to be increasingly common!) I was speaking multiple weekends a month, and Keith was working long hours, and we weren't connecting. A few nights in a row we didn't make love because I was preoccupied. Then I spoke at a conference for three nights. I arrived home in the middle of the night after a long day of travel, so we didn't have sex that night either. The next night I was still tired, so I put on my "no trespassing" flannel pajamas, but neither of us slept well because both of us were feeling that rift. And then—bingo!—the next night we did it.

The following day Keith arrived home with flowers.

Sex flowers.

I got mad. I interpreted it like this: *My husband wants sex too much, so he'll reward me when we make love and punish me when we don't. He'll be deliberately distant when we don't make love so that I will start putting out.* I was really ticked.

After thinking this through, I realized I was attributing to him the kinds of motivations that I often have. And then it hit me: maybe the reason Keith bought me flowers was simply because he felt close to me.

I assumed what was going through his brain was, *I need to manipulate my wife into doing what I want.*

What was really going through Keith's head was, *I love my wife. I think I'll buy her flowers.*

Men don't tend to analyze relationships the same way women do. That means it's often easier to make them content. In general, they need two things: respect and sex. When we affirm what they do and show them appreciation, they feel ten feet tall. When we make love to them, we affirm their manhood and they feel loved. And when they feel loved, they tend to feel less antsy, more compassionate, and more eager to keep pleasing us because they feel that the relationship is something they do well.

Obviously I'm generalizing, but studies have shown repeatedly that it is often easier to make a man feel loved than it is to make a woman feel loved, simply because of the differences in the way men and women think. As Bill and Pam Farrel describe so vividly in their book *Men Are Like Waffles, Women Are Like Spaghetti*, men live their lives mentally in little boxes, like the squares in waffles.[4] They compartmentalize. When they are in their "relationship box," they think about the relationship. When they are in the "work box," they think about work. When they have sex, they're in the "sex box." And when sex is good, they feel good. The box they're in, at this moment, is good, which means that they, at this moment, feel good.

When the box feels good, they'll stay in that box happily. When the box feels bad, they'll retreat. That's why if a man feels he's lousy at marriage, he'll start working more (hanging out in the "work box") or playing on the computer more (hanging out in the "leisure box"). He retreats to his boxes of competence.

We spaghetti creatures, though, are a lot squishier. We live with everything worming its way into everything else. Instead of life being divided up into distinct boxes, it's all interconnected. So if you're upset because your husband seems to lose his temper with little ten-year-old Johnny too much, and then you're out to dinner and your husband does everything right and says you look beautiful and brings you home and kisses you and gives you a massage, you still may resist sex and pull away because the whole time he's doing something nice for you, little Johnny is still in the picture.

He can be so gentle with me. Why can't he do this with Johnny? It's only because he wants sex, isn't it? Johnny is a piece of spaghetti, weaving into all your thoughts, even while on a date.

This propensity of spaghetti to worm its way into everything makes it awfully difficult for men to get us in the mood. (Some women, of course, have much higher libidos than their husbands, and we'll talk about that later in this book, but a big frustration in many marriages is that his libido is higher than hers.) My husband has asked me so many times, "What would it take to get you in the mood?" and I've sat there, stumped.

"A massage would help," I'd say.

So he'd do that, and nope, that wasn't it.

"Maybe talking about what was on my mind earlier in the day would help."

So we'd do that, and that wasn't the magic bullet either.

Keith would get frustrated, because why couldn't I just tell him what he should do? But the simple answer was that I didn't know, since there was always some stray piece of spaghetti upsetting the whole evening—and it was usually a different piece of spaghetti every night.

Women are complex. There's nothing he can do to take care of all that spaghetti. And because we're multitaskers and we think about so many things at once, if even one of those things is off kilter, our mood is often killed.

It is relatively easy for a woman to make a man feel appreciated, because he can experience just one thing at a time. It is relatively hard, though, for a man to make a woman feel loved and appreciated, because she tends to have so much on her mind all at once. *That's why so much of the power for the dynamic of the relationship rests in our hands.*

I love watching older couples hold hands while they walk or look into each other's eyes at restaurants. But every now and then an older couple makes me sad. I met Maude at the local recreation center in an aquafit class, which is populated mostly by women several decades older than me. While most of the women talked nonstop about their grandchildren, Maude would often complain about her husband, Jerry. He's too lazy to come and work out. He never gets the right groceries if she sends him out. He forgot to call his sister on her birthday, and she had to apologize for him. And boy, is he grumpy!

Then Jerry had a minor heart attack, and his doctor told him he had better join a fitness class. When he arrived, I expected to see a surly man who was angry at life. Instead I saw a man with a mischievous smile whose eyes sparkled—except when he looked at Maude. With all the other older ladies he was quickly a favorite. To Maude he was never good enough.

I wonder what Maude and Jerry would look like today if, back in their first few years of marriage, Maude had thanked him for getting the groceries he did get instead of pointing out what he missed? What would have happened if she had respected his opinion, held on to his every word, and cherished their time together? I bet his eyes today would sparkle for her too. If she had acted like his neighbor, instead of concentrating on how hurt she was or how inadequate he had been, could she have created a different relationship?

Action Step: Don't just tell your husband that you love him. Every day, tell him *why* you love him. Instead of focusing on things that irk you, emphasize what you love about him.

GOD WANTS ME TO LOVE MY HUSBAND FIRST

All of this boils down to one thing: what God cares about most is character, and that means God wants us to do the right thing—even if our husbands don't seem to be jumping on the bandwagon yet. After all, we don't do the right thing only after he's done the right thing; we do the right thing simply because it's the right thing. *And that can change everything.*

Taking that first step is a very Jesus-like thing to do. Paul tells us in Romans 5:8 that "while we were still sinners, Christ died for us." Jesus didn't wait for us to clean up our act first; he died when we were still pathetic. And God wants us to reach out and love our husbands now too—even if they're "still sinners."

It's hard to take that first step if you're still justifying your distance and anger because you're heartbroken. My friend Julie has been brokenhearted in her marriage. She was overwhelmed and lonely while raising her two boys, and her logic-loving husband didn't know how to cope with her emotional outbursts. She never experienced a breakthrough until she realized that her broken heart was part of the problem. She said:

> Both of us were fully dedicated Christians, but our marriage was in the tank. I learned during that time that there is a vast difference between having a broken heart and having a broken spirit. I cried a lot, prayed a lot, talked to my husband a lot—but all from a broken heart. It wasn't until I let my spirit be broken—when I truly humbled myself and took a hard look at how God saw ME in our marriage—that I felt the shift. Years later, I can honestly say our marriage is wonderful and ONE-derful!

Sometimes that broken spirit is the only route to true healing in a marriage. When we stop saying, "He's hurting me," and start saying, "How have I contributed to his hurt, and how can I start turning this situation around?" our marriages can change. Humility is an essential ingredient for change. Humility doesn't mean that we accept all the blame; humility simply says that we're willing to take that first step to love our husbands as our neighbors—whether or not they take a similar step toward us. We do what's right because we want to obey God.

> **Action Step:** Make confession and apology a part of your prayer life and your marriage. Start your prayers with confession, and when you know you've done wrong, apologize immediately— even if your husband has done wrong too.

THE FIRST DUTY OF A NEIGHBOR IS KINDNESS

God wants you to be kind to your husband. It really is that simple—and yet also that difficult.

That's a lesson author and blogger Juana Mikels learned when her marriage was in crisis thirty years ago—only two years after she and her husband had walked down the aisle and pledged to love each other forever. Yet she couldn't climb over her mountain of hurt and decided she'd be happier apart from him. Six months into their separation she realized that she had made a mistake. She wanted to reconcile. Terry, though, was gun-shy. Juana had wounded him deeply when she left. How did he know she wouldn't do it again?

Juana decided she would woo him back with kindness. Her first act on moving back into the house was to make him coffee— which he refused before storming out and later moving out himself. That really got her back up. There she was, ready to reach out and humble herself and love him again, and he rejected her peace offering! Wisely, she sought the counsel of an older couple in her church who prayed for her fervently, especially asking God to make her patient and kind toward her husband.

Juana broke through his initial reluctance, and they began dating again, going to a basketball game or out to dinner or out for a walk. Sometimes when he lashed out, testing her resolve, she'd dish it right back.

She told me, "I realized that when I attacked him, I may as well have been cutting off my own leg. We were acting like we were in competition, when we weren't."

They weren't meant to be on opposite sides; they were meant to be on the same side.

The reconciliation process took a year and a half—much longer than Juana wanted. But in that time she learned to value his heart and to care when he was hurting. She listened to the feelings behind his words, rather than reacting with her own feelings. She was kind, and that kindness melted his anger and broke down his defenses.

"We became us again," she said.

Today kindness has become the operating principle of their marriage.

As it says in Proverbs, "Those who are kind reward themselves, but the cruel do themselves harm" (11:17, NRSV).

When you see God as your personal genie and focus only on your own feelings, you miss out on the chance to build the kind of oneness that you ultimately want. Your husband is your neighbor. Treat him as kindly and politely as you would a stranger—with no spaghetti strings attached. And you might find that your broken heart starts to heal.

Action Step: Do two acts of kindness to your husband every day. Need some ideas? You'll find a bunch on page pages 28–30!

When I stopped focusing on what Keith needed to do to make me feel better and looked at how I could show him love, not only my actions changed, but my feelings did too. Believing that "us" was more important than "me" meant that I couldn't keep rehashing old hurts; I had to ask, "What will strengthen us right now?" And the answer was rarely feeling sorry for myself. It was always figuring out how to love my husband more. He is my neighbor, and we are both interconnected. I can't hurt him without hurting me too. But when I bless him, I bless us. And that's what being a neighbor is all about.

Summary of Action Steps

1. How well do you know your husband? Every day for the next two weeks, ask your husband something new about him—and share something about yourself.
2. Show your husband he is your priority. Put on makeup for him, greet him at the door, or kiss him before you kiss anybody else.
3. Tell your husband daily *why* you love him.
4. Make confession part of your prayer life every day— and apologize whenever you feel an inkling that you have done wrong.
5. Practice random acts of kindness. Choose two to three from pages 28–30 to make into habits.

Random Acts of Kindness for My Husband

Need some practical ideas on how to act like your husband's neighbor? Here are twenty-two to get you going. Your husband may not like all of them—if he's an introvert and needs space, for instance, rubbing his shoulders while he's taking time to unwind on the Internet probably won't be interpreted as kind. So read this list through the filter of your husband's preferences and personality. Then choose two or three to get in the habit of doing regularly.

1. Praise him in front of the kids.
2. Make him a coffee to take with him in the morning.
3. Give him a back rub.
4. Brag about him to your friends when he can hear.
5. Tell him one thing you admire about him in relation to his work—and try to think of different things each time.
6. Rub your fingers through his hair as you're watching a movie.
7. Lay out his clothes for him the night before.

8. Make an appointment to get an oil change for the car.

9. Sort the mail so he doesn't have to.

10. Text him and tell him specifically what you love doing with him.

11. Take him a glass of water if he's working out in the heat.

12. Take him a drink when he's working at his desk.

13. Ask him what he'd like for dinner—let him choose the menu at least once a week.

14. Wear something you know he loves.

15. Going out to pick up an ice cream or treat with the kids? Bring him one too—even if you went out during the day when he was at work. Save it for him, with a note saying, "We were thinking of you!"

16. Rub him dry when he gets out of the shower—and put some "manly" moisturizer cream on him or some talcum powder. Towel dry his hair, and tell him you love how he smells. Granted, this one may be a little sexual.

17. Read a chapter of a book, a funny story, or a newspaper article to him while he takes a bath.

18. Pray for him while you're lying in bed—out loud. Reach out, put your arm on his, and say a sentence-or-two prayer.

19. Walking beside him? Reach out and touch him for a second!

20. Rub his feet while you're watching TV. (You can even get a cloth and wash his feet and put some cream on them too.)

21. Ask his advice on something—and then follow it (without challenging him!).

22. Ask him to explain to you something about one of his hobbies.

Thought #2

My Husband
Can't Make Me Mad

You can usually find my friend Derek yanking up trees, bulldozing through rock, or fixing a truck. He's a man's man. But he also loves shopping for clothes for his wife, Lisa. I can still picture Lisa at church one Sunday twelve years ago. She arrived in a gorgeous salmon A-line skirt and blazer with a ruched blouse. Lisa's a farm girl, so the put-together ensemble took me by surprise.

"You look awesome," I gushed, perhaps a little more enthusiastically than was polite.

"I know!" she said. "Derek picked it out for our anniversary."

Every year he buys her a new outfit. He has a knack for knowing what will fit her and what will flatter her—even better than Lisa can choose herself.

Around five years ago, though, Derek took a job that keeps him away from home, condensing most of their couple time to the weekends. Recently, when Lisa needed a new outfit for a business meeting, she drove to the local mall by herself, gritted her teeth, and picked out the least terrible one she could find.

When Derek arrived home that weekend, he noticed the new clothes. "I could have picked you out something even better."

Lisa's blood pressure rose. *I know Derek shops better than I do, but it isn't my fault that I have to do everything around here while he's gone! It's not my fault that we don't have enough time to shop anymore. I did my best.*

"It's so silly," Lisa told me on the phone. "I know he misses shopping for me. He loves feeling like he's pampered me, and he's just disappointed he doesn't get the chance. But at the time it just made me so teed off."

When we feel disappointed in our mates, we often think that our emotional response is out of our control. We picture ourselves perfectly innocent, when out of the blue our husbands send us reeling. They tick us off, and we feel angry. We feel hurt. But what if this isn't inevitable? Christian philosopher Peter Kreeft said, "Feelings, like waves, look more substantial than they are,"[1] and I think he's right. What if feelings don't need to automatically have that much power over what we think?

I remember watching my daughter Rebecca, when she was three, grappling with waves on her first trip to the ocean. She'd fall and get sucked underwater and come up spluttering and crying. And then my husband would pick her up and show her how to withstand those waves.

"All you have to do, Becca," he'd say, "is dig in deeper, face the waves, and watch for them."

With fierce determination Rebecca would wiggle her toes to dig her feet firmly into the sand, squint with concentration at the waves, and then laugh as she was able to roll with them. Prepare for it, and the wave becomes a minor bump, not something that leaves us winded. Marriage gives us the same challenge. It's easy for feelings to bowl us over, but it isn't inevitable.

Thought #2:
My husband can't make me mad.

Now I'm not trying to downplay real feelings of hurt or anger. You may have substantial issues to deal with in your marriage, and in the upcoming chapters we'll look at how to resolve those conflicts. Often when we're ticked off, though, it's more for the reason Lisa felt mad at Derek: life happens, and we let ourselves get carried along.

TAKE EVERY THOUGHT CAPTIVE

If his behavior is irritating, though, doesn't keeping our cool sound like an awfully tall order? The apostle Paul didn't think so. In 2 Corinthians 10:5 he said, "We demolish arguments and every pretension that sets itself up against the knowledge of God, *and we take captive every thought to make it obedient to Christ.*"

Instead of letting our thoughts determine our feelings and our actions, we can *choose* to determine what to do with our thoughts. We don't have to let them bowl us over.

That's the biblical view of the mind: we take an active role in choosing which thoughts to entertain. And in this chapter I want to show you how you can make that a reality in your own life.

Before we do that, though, I want to make it clear what I am *not* saying. I've often heard a pat answer that goes something like this:

> **Pat Answer:** *Don't take offense! If someone is insensitive or hurtful, overlook it and keep your focus on God.*

Hear something that bugs you? Just ignore it!

"Don't sweat the small stuff" is generally good advice. Most annoyances are just small things—such as which way you load the toilet paper roll or how you squeeze the toothpaste. But since not all things are small, not all things can be ignored, and not all things *should* slide off your back. I am certainly not suggesting that you ignore genuine threats to your marriage. You must notice big things and deal with them, as we'll talk about later.

But we can deliberately change our thought patterns so the little things are much less likely to bother us. To do this, I suggest we take our thoughts captive in a two-pronged approach: (1) we vigilantly look out for when feelings are likely to overwhelm us; (2) we deliberately think about our marriages in positive ways.

Step 1: Identify the Trigger Points

As I shared earlier, my husband and I have periods of busyness where his call schedule and work schedule conflict with my speaking schedule, and suddenly we can go from eating together every night to seeing each other only a few nights over a span of a few weeks. I've even stopped calling them periods of busyness and started calling them seasons of distance. When we don't share day-to-day together, life gets more isolated, even if we try to compensate with phone calls and texts and Skype.

When Keith comes home, even though I'm glad he's back, I feel as if it's almost a disruption. I have to cook full meals again, rather than grabbing what I want on the go. I can't work when an idea strikes me. Because my schedule has to readjust, when I watch him come home and play a game on his computer, I overreact. I've spent all this time gearing up to do something with him, and then he ignores me! It doesn't matter that he never plays for more than half an hour and that I normally don't mind him unwinding. If I have to get with the program, shouldn't he have to also?

That "season of distance" is my trigger for feeling ticked off. If we hadn't been enduring distance, his playing a game wouldn't annoy me. After all, I've got my own time wasters! But when I'm already feeling distant, my emotions take over. When something else is affecting our mood already, we're at much higher risk of becoming ticked off. That "something else" is our trigger for major irritation.

If you're not sure how trigger points work, look at these different scenarios. One night your husband arrives home later than he was supposed to, and it doesn't bother you one bit. Yet a week later he walks in the door equally late, and you've already been seething for half an hour, rehearsing the speech you'll launch into once he steps inside. You think, *He doesn't care about our family!* You decide that he has the problem—or even, that he *is* the problem.

Or maybe some mornings you're ready to tear your husband's hair out for leaving his socks on the floor instead of pitching them in the hamper, while other mornings you happily fetch the offending garments while humming to yourself.

We dwell on the particular infraction—being late or leaving socks lying around—but we often fail to realize that it isn't necessarily what our husbands do that makes us mad; it's other things that are going on in the background that cause us to see our husbands in a bad light. We let these other things—these triggers—influence how we think about our husbands. By scanning for these triggers, though, we can minimize their ability to send our thoughts reeling.

Be on the lookout for these four common triggers:

Feeling Overwhelmed/Busy. Let's say that the night your husband came in half an hour late and you exploded was also the night that one child had soccer practice at 6:45 while another child had swimming lessons at 7:00, and all day you had obsessed over how to get each child to the right place at the right time without making anybody late. You had no leeway for error.

Something to Consider: Ask yourself, *The last few times that I've become frustrated with my spouse, have I been extremely busy?* If so, maybe you should take a look at your schedule—

kids' activities, extra work projects, church activities—and see in what areas you can cut back or ask for help.

Feeling Tired. When we're exhausted, we get grumpy. My friend Tammy had just landed in the Quebec City airport after a trip to Scotland, and her husband was standing at Arrivals, waiting to hug her and welcome her home. Jet-lagged after more than twenty-four hours with very little sleep, she collapsed in the car, looking forward to falling into bed as soon as she arrived home. But during that car ride, her husband, Steve, mentioned the fact that Revenue Canada (Canada's equivalent to America's IRS) had decided to audit her tuition receipts from the degree she'd been pursuing.

And so began an hour-long tiff about whose fault it was that the receipts had not been sent in, whether it was urgent to talk about then, and how stressed everyone was.

"I said things to Steve I would never normally say," Tammy admitted to me sheepishly. "But I wasn't myself. I was all foggy."

The next morning she dug out the receipt in question, scanned it, and faxed it to Revenue Canada. The whole process took thirty seconds. But her exhaustion blew it up to an hour-long blame game the day before. When we are tired, we just don't handle little things as well.

Something to Consider: Ask yourself, *Have I been getting enough sleep lately?* If not, identify the root cause of your lack of sleep. Do you need to head to bed earlier? Get off of the computer earlier in the evening? Train the children to go to bed easily, without all the time-consuming drama? Reduce things on your plate so you have more time to sleep? Buy earplugs if your husband snores? Make a plan for increasing your sleep so you are better rested during the day.

Feeling Defensive. Maybe you're angry at yourself because you can't seem to keep up with the housework. Maybe you feel as if you should be further ahead in your career. Maybe you feel that you should be a better mother.

When speaking at a conference recently, a woman approached me for prayer because she found that she was constantly angry at her kids. She didn't want to be the kind of mom who always yelled, but the house was messy, loud, and chaotic, and she found herself constantly grumpy.

As we talked, I shared with her that anger is usually a secondary emotion. We react in anger because we feel something else first, and if that feeling is too sensitive or too difficult to deal with, we deflect it into anger. In her case, she had an immense fear of failure. She was afraid that she wasn't a good mom and was a lousy homemaker. When things around the house became frenzied, that seemed to prove her fear was justified, so she became angry instead to avoid the guilt.

The problem, though, was that she was already angry at herself. And when we're angry at ourselves, we usually deflect that anger toward other people, because it's psychologically easier.

Something to Consider: Ask yourself, *Am I trying too hard to be perfect? Do I constantly feel like a failure?* If so, commit to praying honestly and vulnerably about your fears. Also work through those concerns with a friend/mentor so that you don't project your anger at yourself onto other people.

Feeling Hormonal. Finally, let's not forget hormones. If I were to track all the times that I've been a crying mess in front of my husband in the last few months, they would line up almost exactly with . . . Well, you know what I'm talking about. And believe me, this gets way worse when you hit your forties and perimenopause starts. Your hormones used to pop up and wave at you every now and then, but now they're tackling you, knocking you down, and stomping on you for good measure.

One day his sock on the floor is just a sock. The next day that sock is Evil Incarnate. So to help me keep a look out for this trigger point, I've downloaded a cycle tracker app[2] on my phone that charts my moodiness and warns me when my bad days are coming. Those are the days now when I retreat and try to spend some time by myself, we order takeout for dinner, and we eat while watching a movie instead of while talking around the dinner table as a family. It's just safer for everyone!

Something to Consider: Ask yourself, *Do I become angry or moody around my monthly cycle?* If so, maybe it's time to plan ahead and mark those difficult times on a calendar, then warn people beforehand.

How to Stop Triggers from Derailing Your Thoughts

1. Think back to the last three times you reacted in anger toward your husband. Were any of these four triggers—feeling overwhelmed/busy, tired, defensive, or hormonal—in play?

2. If you can't remember the circumstances surrounding the last few times you've been angry, get a notebook and keep track throughout the next month. Whenever you start to feel angry, take a step back and ask yourself if any of these triggers are affecting you.

3. If one particular trigger keeps rearing its head, brainstorm with your husband (or a friend) about how to reduce the impact of that trigger.

Step 2: Choose What to Think

Once you've identified your trigger points for aggravation, it's much easier to avoid feeling ticked off altogether! But there's something else you can do to reduce the chances of feeling ticked off: deliberately think about stuff that makes you happy. Paul addressed this idea in Philippians 4:8:

Whatever is true, whatever is noble, whatever is right,
whatever is pure, whatever is lovely, whatever is admirable—
if anything is excellent or praiseworthy—think about
such things.

Taking thoughts captive involves being deliberate about what
we choose to fill our minds with. Life doesn't have to be a free-
form stream of consciousness, where any thought that comes into
our heads is entertained. Thinking can be an intentional and deliberate exercise.

And this works too! It may sound far-fetched—especially
when you wonder, *How can I think about the good and the admirable when I'm really upset?* Yet when Paul penned those words,
he was sitting inside a prison, being guarded 24/7. He knew he
was facing almost certain death. Regardless of what you're going
through, it's hard to compare it with that. And yet if you were to
do a study of the book of Philippians, you'd find that the words
Paul wrote most often were *joy* and *rejoice.* The theme of Philippians is about learning to rejoice!

Right before Paul asked us to think about the pure and the
right and the admirable, he wrote,

Rejoice in the Lord always. I will say it again: Rejoice! Let
your gentleness be evident to all. The Lord is near. Do not
be anxious about anything, but in every situation, by
prayer and petition, with thanksgiving, present your
requests to God. And the peace of God, which transcends

all understanding, will guard your hearts and your minds in Christ Jesus." (Philippians 4:4–7)

No matter our circumstances, our primary response should be to rejoice. Certainly if we have problems we are to take them to God, but then we're promised that the peace of God will guard our hearts—*and our minds.* Peace involves both our feelings and our thoughts. And Paul tells us how to renew those thoughts: think about the good things. I believe that we can deliberately apply this in our marriages too.

Catch Him Doing Good. My friend Sharol Josephson is co-director of FamilyLife Canada, and we speak frequently together at conferences. In her parenting talk, she relates how she learned early on with her sons that if she wanted to mold their behavior to look like Jesus, she had to be proactive. Sharol deliberately started looking for anything they did that was praiseworthy, and then she'd point it out to them. "I noticed that you saw when your teammate felt left out and you went over and included him in the conversation. That made me so proud of you." Or perhaps, "I noticed that you didn't let yourself get riled up when your brother was poking you today, but you just went quietly to your room. You're learning well how to avoid getting angry." Sharol noticed the things they did well and then spoke them out loud. And her boys thrived.

That got me thinking about marriage. *What if we made it a habit to catch our husbands doing good?*

When Shaunti Feldhahn was first researching differences between the genders, she discovered that a man's heart cry is to feel that "you see what I did on the outside, and you think it's good." A woman's cry, on the other hand, is to know that "you see me on the inside, and you think it's good." We need different things. Other people have also found this love/respect dynamic, where women desperately want to feel loved, but men desperately want that respect.[3] The problem for Shaunti personally was that love seemed a lot easier to communicate. It's simple to say "I love you," or to reach out and hold a hand. She tried saying "I respect you" to her husband, but that didn't have the same effect and they both agreed it seemed odd.[4]

A few years later, though, when she was doing research for her book *The Surprising Secrets of Highly Happy Marriages,* she discovered what men need to hear—and it's so simple. Men need to be told "thank you." Shaunti wrote, "A woman's saying 'Thank you' to her man is the emotional equivalent of his saying 'I love you' to her."[5] Just notice things he does—and then say thank you.[6]

Action Step: Start "catching" your husband doing good! At least once a day thank your husband for something specific he has done.

We See What We're Looking For. Medical personnel will often tell you that there's something to the "full moon" phenomenon. On nights when there's a full moon, the emergency room tends to fill up with bizarre cases. My husband, Keith, an analytical sort of physician, doesn't buy this explanation. Whenever a paramedic or a nurse or another doc starts mentioning the "full moon effect," he launches into a certain rant that he's perfected, which goes something like this:

> Let's say that one night you're on duty and instead of heart attacks, broken bones, and strokes, most patients need help because of bar fights or poison ivy in the nether regions. You happen to glance out the window and don't notice anything peculiar. But during one shift you're inundated with more bar fights, and you look out the window, and you see a full moon! Because you were looking for the full moon, you noticed it. The other times when you didn't see one, its absence didn't register. Emergency rooms can be just as bizarre every night, but we still tend to think the full moon does something peculiar because we're scanning for it.

When you look for something, you will find it. So are we expecting the good or the bad from our husbands? I recently posted this status update on Facebook, complaining about how women seem to expect their husbands to be immature:

> Just saw a graphic that said: "Your husband will always be your biggest and oldest child who requires the most adult supervision." Why is it okay to talk about men in these derogatory terms?

Most people agreed with my sentiment, but a surprising number said something like, "It's not derogatory; it's just gently teasing or endearing." Or else they wrote, "Maybe we just need to lighten up and see the funny side!" And then a few said, "My husband *is* a big child!"

Let's be careful with what we joke about, because even if we intend to be funny, a part of our brain is still telling ourselves, *My husband is irresponsible. My husband isn't serious. I have to baby my husband.*

When you tell yourself that, you will notice the things he does that live up to that stereotype. My aquafit buddies Jerry and Maude were living embodiments of this (see Thought #1 for their full story). Maude talked about Jerry as if he were a child—complaining about how when she was sick they had to live on hard-boiled eggs since he couldn't cook, and how in fifty years he had never done laundry. Maude may have felt superior, but their marriage certainly paid the price.

When we look for the bad, we'll see the bad. But this can work to our advantage too. When we choose to look for the good things our husbands do, we also tend to notice those things more. In fact, we'll notice them so much that we often will fail to notice when they do things that are more likely to tick us off.

And that's how God created our minds to work. *Whatever we focus on expands.* If you focus on God's goodness and on being thankful for your marriage, you will tend to notice the things that you have to be grateful about. When you focus on the things that bug you, you will tend to feel significantly more bugged.

Action Step: Don't joke about men being inferior. Stop laughing at jokes that as a whole paint men in a bad light.

I Can Choose Not to Criticize

Twenty-nine-year-old Ruby had four kids under five. Life, to put it simply, was über-chaotic, and she often found herself frustrated with her husband, who didn't have to juggle the constant demands of the house and the kids the way that she did. Then she chose to stop being constantly ticked off. Here's Ruby's story in her own words:

A couple years ago I realized that I couldn't look at my husband without seeing everything wrong with him. I was constantly annoyed, irritated, and disappointed.

I must have prayed about becoming more loving because God dropped an idea into my brain. I would stop criticizing Dave for one whole month. In order to keep from falling off the wagon, I decided to write about it. Every day. On Facebook, for all my friends to see. They would be my accountability group, whether they wanted to or not.

When I told Dave my plan, I was so nervous. I thought he'd roll his eyes or be suspicious. Instead, he beamed. And another little piece of my heart broke. I hadn't realized how hurt he'd been by my bad attitude, sarcastic remarks, and snide comments—my passive-aggressive attempts to fix him.

I found that, because I wasn't allowed to say anything snide to him, I stopped thinking critical things too. It happened gradually. I'd start a rant in my head about his leaving his side of the bed unmade or his floor all messy, and then I'd stop. All the nasty comments I was saving in my head for him were useless, since I wasn't allowed to say them. So I stopped searching for them.

Since I was required to say nice things, I had to look for them: reasons I was thankful, things he was doing right. And slowly, I saw him differently. I realized that all those negative things were really coming from my own baggage, my own selfishness, and my own needs and desperation. They weren't the whole truth.

Once my mouth, and more especially my thoughts, got out of the way, I realized I had a great husband. By the end of the month, I had formed a new habit. And as an added bonus, I'd had great conversations with my friends on Facebook, and I think we all grew a little.

After shutting up about my own needs and stopping thinking me, me, ME! all the time, I realized I had some issues of my own I needed to work through. I had no concept of boundaries and saying no. I had no idea that a "good Christian wife" could ask her husband in a nice, non-ragey way to please put his lunch bag away instead of stewing over feeling like his maid for months and then exploding in a vague storm of emotions and frustration.

I had a lot to learn, but the month of no criticizing was a great first step for me.[7]

When Ruby focused on being grateful and silenced the criticisms, her whole perspective changed. Interestingly, her husband didn't become perfect. She had just developed a healthier view of him—and a healthier way to handle conflict too.

Action Step: For one week, do not say anything critical to or about your spouse.

BELIEVE THE BEST

You can watch for your triggers and choose to be grateful and catch your husband doing good—but in every marriage, inevitably he will do something that disappoints you or frustrates you. What do you do then?

My friend Mollie and her husband, Craig, slept naked for the first few years of their marriage—until kids came along and awkwardness took over. These days when Mollie goes to bed in nothing but her birthday suit, she's sending a strong signal that something's gonna happen.

After a grueling week dealing with their oldest daughter's crises from her first month away at college and a parent's preparation for chemotherapy, Mollie decided to send that signal, which to her was unmistakable. Though Craig and she were both exhausted, she thought they'd get a good night's sleep first and then "something" would happen in the morning. So she tucked herself under the covers, cuddled up to her husband, and drifted off wearing only a smile.

In the morning when she awoke at the crack of dawn, she noticed Craig sneaking out of the room. In his hunting clothes.

With a rifle. Duck hunting had taken precedence over her in her birthday suit.

"At first I was really ticked," Mollie told me. "Did he not find me attractive anymore? Did he not want to spend time with me after all we had been through that week? But then I realized I was being silly. Of course Craig didn't care about duck hunting more than sex. He was just unwinding his way, and we'd unwind our way later that night, and in the meantime, I got to sleep in!" Changing her thoughts helped her focus more rationally on the truth and helped her take back control of the emotions that threatened to drive a wedge in their relationship.

When our husbands do something that could be interpreted as a negative, we have two choices. We can accept the interpretation that validates our anger, or we can choose to be generous and believe the best.

"Believing the best" was one of the best predictors of a happy marriage, Shaunti Feldhahn found. According to Shaunti's studies, in highly happy couples, 99 percent of survey respondents said they do care about their spouses and want the best for them, even during painful times.[8]

The message to take from this? Your spouse is not out to get you. Your spouse is not trying to insult you, make you miserable, or hurt you. When you hear something that hurts you, it's best to back up and remind yourself, *My husband does want the best for me.*

The fact that your husband cares for you is not what really makes the difference, though. It's you believing it to be true. In struggling marriages, 80 percent of people still want the best for their mates, even during painful times. The kicker, however, is that only 59 percent of people in struggling marriages believe it.[9] It's that misunderstanding—not believing your spouse wants the best for you—that often makes the struggle worse.

Action Step: The next time you start to feel angry, ask yourself, *What's the most generous interpretation of why my husband did that or said that?*

LET THOSE LITTLE THINGS GO

It's easy to let little things tick us off and start the cycle where we each blow up at the other until everyone becomes unhappy. But we should never give little things that much power.

Kia, now forty, has been married eight years to her army husband, who has been deployed twice since they wed. Her story helps me to keep perspective when I find myself getting upset with my husband. She told me:

> The little things used to drive me nuts—boots in the living room, empty milk jug in the fridge, soaking wet bathroom after a shower. Aghhh! But when he's gone, I long to complain about the water on the floor. I long to trip over his boots on the rug or complain about him snacking in the middle of the night and leaving crumbs everywhere. I always whisper a "thank you" when my socks get wet from walking in the bathroom after he's

showered. I know he's home. And I know too many wives who can't say that.

Shaunti Feldhahn loves to spread the word: "As simple as it sounds, if we want to have happy marriages, we must choose to boss our feelings around."[10] If it's a little thing, let it be a little thing. *You don't need to feel ticked off.* It's so much nicer—and freeing!—to choose to feel gratitude and love for your husband instead.

Summary of Action Steps

1. Identify your most common triggers for conflict. Keep track of them and then strategize ways to reduce them.
2. Catch your husband doing good—and thank him for it.
3. Stop laughing or sharing any jokes that are derogatory of men.
4. For one week, do not say anything critical about your spouse.
5. The next time you start to feel angry, ask yourself, *What's the most generous interpretation of why my husband did that or said that?*

Thought #3

My Husband Was Not Put on This Earth to Make Me Happy

When I was a teenager crying into my pillow over the latest heartbreak, I'd make this promise to myself: "One day, Sheila, someone will love you perfectly."

After having both my father and my stepfather leave me in my childhood, and then a string of guys in high school and university decide that I just wasn't worth the commitment, I was sure that I deserved true love. I had suffered enough; my time would come! And if God blesses marriage, then I was certain he wanted me to experience that boundless love with a wonderful husband too.

Today I do have a man who loves and cherishes me, but that love was once tainted because he broke off our initial engagement. And as I shared with you earlier, when rejection or criticism rear their ugly heads in other areas of my life, often the sadness of old rejections washes over me again. Yet it isn't only the rejection that sends me reeling; it's that the rejection triggers the disappointment that I will never, in this life, have a man who will always love me perfectly. When these moods strike, I begin to catalog the failings of every man in my life—even my husband who now treats me like a princess. No matter what he does, he can never make up for disappointing me over two decades ago. He didn't give me that fairy tale love that every little girl deserves.

Can you see how that kind of attitude can hurt a marriage?

I've only had a few bad bouts of "poor, poor, pitiful me" during my marriage, and I hope I've silenced them for good now, because when those bouts hit, they're totally counterproductive. The more I fixate on how I deserved my perfect fairy tale, the more I realize I don't have it. And I make myself miserable—even though I'm with a wonderful, thoughtful man today. That's why happiness is like a boomerang: if you aim for happiness, expecting that fairy tale, those expectations will come back and smack you.

Is Happiness Really the Point?

The fairy tale of happily-ever-after gets dangled enticingly in front of us from Disney movies, hit songs, and romance novels. Then we grow up and have babies who don't sleep; husbands who seem to want only one thing; and careers that are impossible to juggle with sick children, day-care schedules, and gymnastics lessons. Where is all this happiness we were promised?

Our religious pat answer feeds right into this, and it goes something like this:

Pat Answer: *God wants to bless his children. If you aren't receiving the blessings, you aren't praying hard enough or clinging close enough to God. Go get your blessing!*

I often wonder what Chinese Christians or Middle Eastern Christians must think of Christians in the Western world. They know that the pursuit of happiness and comfort is not God's primary concern—it never has been. Every single one of the apostles met gruesome fates, except for John, but even he died in exile. God is interested in bringing the world to himself, not in giving us a comfortable life here so that we don't need him. We have taken our culture's "you deserve happiness" message and put a Christian spin on it. It sounds lovely, but it really leads to disenchantment with our marriages and with God.

Perhaps we're aiming for the wrong thing. After all, I can't think of a worse route to marital happiness than always to be wondering if I've achieved it. If I'm constantly asking myself, "Am I happy?" I will always find reasons why I'm not. *My husband works too many long hours. He doesn't take the kids enough to give me time to myself. He can't figure out what a mop is for.*

Thought #3:
My husband was not put on this earth to make me happy.

If you're constantly saying to yourself, "I'll be happy when . . . ," and you can fill in the blank, then chances are you never will be happy in your marriage. If your husband suddenly did the thing you wished for, you'd simply wish for something else in its place. That's the nature of the quest for happiness. It's rooted in circumstances, and it makes you a passive recipient of what happens to you. That's why aiming for happiness will tend to backfire, especially in marriage.

God Didn't Make a Soul Mate for Me

We often assume happiness is God's goal for marriage because we hear things like this:

> Pat Answer: *God has a perfect will for your life, and that includes a soul mate who will complete you.*

This idea of a soul mate permeates popular culture. L. J. Smith, author of *The Vampire Diaries,* described a soul mate like this: "You don't love a girl because of beauty. You love her because she sings a song only you can understand."[1] Romance writer Rainbow Rowell put it like this in her bestseller *Eleanor & Park:* "What were the chances you'd ever meet someone like that? he wondered. Someone you could love forever, someone who would forever love you back? And what did you do when that person was born half a world away? The math seemed impossible."[2]

The soul mate promise says that each of us has only one person to complete us, and they're out there, waiting for fate to step in and bring us together. Christians have even put our own slant on soul mates: God has a perfect plan for your life, and that includes the perfect person for you to marry, who matches you in every way.

It sounds romantic, but is it true?

My grandfather had great luck in love but horrible luck with cancer. He loved three women wholeheartedly and passionately in his life: my grandmother, whom he was with for twenty-five years before she died of a brain tumor; the woman I called "Nana," who died seventeen years into their marriage; and Dorothy, the woman who beamed with pride at my wedding and who left him a widower for the last time. Each woman was totally unique, yet he loved them all. And in his last years he had photos of all three of them in his living room: the three loves of his life. Was only one his soul mate? If so, which one?

Telling people that there is only one perfect person for them—one person God has specially selected and made for them—implies there is also a promise that this person will make them happy all the time and in every way. They match perfectly, so they should find perfect bliss together.

When we buy into that mind-set, though, and when the fairy tale doesn't live up to its promise, we start to blame our husband. Maybe he wasn't our soul mate after all.

In *The Sacred Search,* Gary Thomas lays out a convincing case that marriage is not about marrying the right person, but about becoming the right person. He encourages us: "Men and women, find a partner with whom you can seek first the kingdom of God, someone who inspires you toward righteousness, and when you do, 'all these things will be added to you.'"[3]

Of course you can be happy in marriage, but that happiness is "added to us" not when we think we deserve it or expect someone else to produce it, but instead when we commit to seeking God and following him.[4] When two people love each other sacrificially, they will find happiness. If they aim for happiness instead of aiming to love, they will ultimately fail to achieve either.

BEING "TRUE TO MYSELF" DOESN'T BRING HAPPINESS

A few years ago Al and Tipper Gore split up, and at the time I remember with dismay how many newspapers chose to put a "happy" spin on it. Deirdre Bair, writing in the *New York Times,* urged us "not to feel sad" about the end of the forty-year union. Instead, we should "rejoice" that they have decided to take the plunge and find themselves![5]

Self-actualization is the new god. But living by your feelings makes you into a liar. If your purpose is to ensure you are always true to your feelings, then you won't be true to anyone else. Al and Tipper vowed at their wedding to love each other "until death do us part," forsaking all others. At least one of them violated that pledge.

Feelings are not the best guide to right and wrong. The world is full of scars from people doing what feels good. As God said in Jeremiah 17:9, "The heart is deceitful above all things and beyond cure. Who can understand it?"

Throughout the Bible, God tells us what we should aim for, and interestingly, feelings and happiness aren't mentioned. Two of my favorite "encapsulations" of God's purposes for us are found in Romans 8:29 and Micah 6:8.

In Romans 8:29, after telling us that God works all things together for good to those who love God, Paul said, "For those God foreknew he also predestined to be conformed to the image of his Son, that he might be the firstborn among many brothers and sisters."

I love the beautiful word picture in this verse. Ultimately, God's main purpose for us is that we are to be "conformed to the image of his Son." He wants us to look more and more like Jesus! That's the purpose of our lives: to look like Christ.

Back in the Old Testament, there's another verse I've always loved about our purpose. Micah 6:8 says, "He has shown you, O mortal, what is good. And what does the LORD require of you? To act justly and to love mercy and to walk humbly with your God."

We're to do what's right (focus on justice); we're to love mercy (focus on grace); and we're to pursue a relationship with God.

That's the purpose of your life, but that should also be the purpose of your marriage. Your marriage is not about happiness; your marriage is about both of you looking more and more like Jesus every day as you both do what is right. You'll demonstrate mercy, forgiving each other as Christ forgave you. You'll shower blessings on each other. But you'll also stand up for justice, believing that looking like Jesus means that you stand for truth. When you do that, it's quite likely that you'll find happiness too.

THE ROUTE TO HAPPINESS RUNS THROUGH JOY

Happiness, though, is a funny word, especially in Christian circles. It often gets a bad rap because it's associated with circumstances rather than faith. Prominent Christian writers such as C. S. Lewis went to great pains to distinguish joy from happiness. Joy, said Lewis, is like experiencing a flash of heaven, almost a "stab," says Lewis, where the clouds are rolled back for a split second and your heart expands and you feel God. It's momentous, and it's big. Happiness, on the other hand, is small and rooted in circumstances here on earth.[6]

Other writers have stressed the difference between happiness and contentment. The apostle Paul, for instance, didn't write very much about happiness, but he did write about contentment:

> I am not saying this because I am in need, for I have
> learned to be content whatever the circumstances. I know
> what it is to be in need, and I know what it is to have
> plenty. I have learned the secret of being content in any
> and every situation, whether well fed or hungry, whether
> living in plenty or in want. I can do all this through him
> who gives me strength. (Philippians 4:11–13)

Perhaps I'm being oversensitive about words, but I do think they matter. Let me suggest this: joy is an emotion that looks upward; contentment is an emotion that looks inward; and happiness is an emotion that looks outward. Joy says, "How great is our God!" Contentment says, "It is well with my soul." And happiness says, "What a wonderful husband I have!"

Happiness is important. We all want to enjoy our marriages. But the ability to enjoy marriage depends first and foremost on our perspective. And what determines that? Our attitude toward God (looking upward) and our heart attitude (looking inward). When we have joy and contentment, happiness in marriage will become much more attainable.

I think that's what David was promising in Psalm 37:4, when he wrote, "Take delight in the LORD, and he will give you the desires of your heart." A quick reading of that seems to imply that if we delight in God, we'll get everything we want. But I don't think that's what David meant. I think he meant that when we delight in God, God actually *gives us our desires*. He changes our heart so that we desire the right things. Our ability to be happy with our marriages, then, depends first and foremost on our ability to delight in God himself. It's like the plaque my hairdresser hung in her shop: "Happiness is having what you want and wanting what you have." When we chase after God first, we'll find that we actually want what he has given us.

Action Step: How's your joy-meter? Add a psalm and a praise song to the beginning of every day. Say thank you to God before you even get out of bed. Sing your praises to God in the shower!

IF I'M UNHAPPY, HE'LL THINK HE NEEDS TO FIX IT

In Thought #1 I talked about how it's often easier for us to turn the marriage around and make it less stressful than it is for our husbands to do so because men live their lives in boxes, compartmentalized, much more than we do. But whether or not a box is a "good" box largely depends on how that box makes our husbands feel. Since one of a man's biggest motivators is feeling competent, he will enjoy the parts of his life that he has under control, and he will likely avoid boxes that make him feel like a failure.

That's why your husband, if he's like most men, likely wants to fix things for you: he wants to feel competent and in control. If you are unhappy, he will feel as though it's his job to fix it—even if the reason you're unhappy has nothing to do with him. If he can't fix it, then he'll feel like a failure and withdraw.

A few years ago, I was feeling overwhelmed by too many demands—homeschooling, writing, speaking. One night, I decided to list to Keith every little thing that was bugging me, including my frustration that I couldn't get our daughter Katie to practice piano, and the fact that she and her sister were squabbling more than usual (although these were minor issues compared to the rest on my plate). Keith's work was flexible, so he offered to homeschool the girls the next day.

Keith started his day with the girls by pulling a sergeant-major routine and reading them the riot act. They were causing their mother stress and they needed to smarten up.

Hearing this tension from my home office, I rushed to run interference for the girls. If he wanted to help, I told him, he wouldn't yell at the girls because the girls weren't my main problem. But he had figured, *If my wife has a problem, I have to fix it.* And since the only things on my long list of complaints that he could actually do something about were the girls' lack of enthusiasm for practicing piano and their excess enthusiasm for fighting, he decided that's what he would zero in on.

I was angry at Keith for being so hard on the girls, he was mad at me for being mad at him when he was just trying to help, and the girls were just flabbergasted.

When we were both finally ready to talk, we realized we had

overreacted. He was genuinely trying to help. But he needed to know that sometimes I just had to vent. I didn't need him to fix anything; I just wanted him to listen. I also had to learn something. When I am unhappy, Keith will automatically feel as if he needs to fix it. My unhappiness has a domino effect on our relationship.

Action Step: The next time you share your stress with your husband, be clear about what you want from him. Before you start explaining the situation, tell him one of these three things: I want you to listen; I want you to run with this and fix it; or I want you to brainstorm with me to help me figure out how to fix it.

My Unhappiness Hurts My Husband

I experienced a similar scenario during the year leading up to writing this book. I had one of the worst years since my son passed away eighteen years ago, and it was all because of hormones. I'm in my early forties. I thought I had a few decades ahead of me before I started feeling old. But this year everything hit me all at once.

First my cycle got out of whack. I've always been a thirty-day kind of gal, like clockwork. When I went to twenty-eight days, I was disappointed, but I knew it was nothing to complain about. Twenty-one days, on the other hand, is absolutely ridiculous. And having to sleep on top of a towel in case Niagara Falls hit was really frustrating.

But that wasn't all. My body started producing fewer red

blood cells, because really, what was the point? I was losing them so fast anyway. Little by little, I lost energy. And then one day the balance tipped, and I woke up so tired I felt as though I was in my first trimester of pregnancy again. Nevertheless, I kept going, until after returning from another speaking trip, I started crying uncontrollably because life was too overwhelming.

This prompted my husband to march me off to the lab with that blood-work requisition that had been sticking to our fridge for the previous six months. Lo and behold, I had major anemia. I wasn't going crazy; I was just depleted.

I downed iron supplements for a few months, happily contented because soon this would all be over. When I went for another checkup — *wham!* — I was even more anemic than before.

Over the next few months I had more tests, became far too intimate with a probe, had adverse reactions to medication that made me think I had bedbugs, and had a varicose vein attack that rendered me immobile for two weeks. But finally my doctor scheduled some surgery to help alleviate some of my issues, and the recovery from this long road of exhaustion, grumpiness, and hormonal ridiculousness could begin.

I know my health concerns pale in comparison to those faced by some women. When my mother was my age, she had surgery for breast cancer. I have much to be thankful for. Yet I also know that this year took a huge toll on my health, my energy, and my mood.

And because of that, it took a huge toll on my husband. He couldn't fix anything, yet he was always looking for something he should be doing differently. He became paranoid around me, afraid to say the wrong thing in case he set me off, which made me upset that he was being so distant. He stopped sharing his own stresses with me, not wanting to add to mine, and that distance increased. We should have been clinging to each other and bearing each other's burdens, but instead we suffered a rift in our relationship because I allowed my mood to dictate how I would respond to him. That's when I learned this important truth: *my contentment is a tremendous gift to give my husband.*

TAKING RESPONSIBILITY FOR MY CONTENTMENT HELPS MY MARRIAGE

We're responsible for our own contentment. That's something my friend Julie had to learn the hard way.

"Our marriage was never fabulous," she told me. "And it went down substantially when we had kids." Her first child was extremely colicky. Her second baby was born prematurely and was on a heart monitor for six months. She'd not anticipated how difficult motherhood would be, and it threw her for a loop.

"I was completely out of my element, and I kept expecting my husband to fix it," Julie said. But her husband was out of his element too. Although he had the job world under control, he didn't know how to step in and control the home front. Julie explained:

> I felt like he wasn't helping me, but he didn't know what
> to do any more than I did. I was trying to make him into
> my savior, and he wasn't my savior. He was supposed to

be my partner. Meanwhile, he was feeling overwhelmed in a different way. His wife had become a complete mess. "Where's the beautiful wife I married?" he'd say. And I was blaming him for making her disappear.

When I was a personal mess, my husband tried to fix it. When it wasn't fixable, he wanted to step away. It just made him feel badly. He didn't know how to react to me.

The more Julie's husband stepped away, the more Julie started to notice all the ways that he wasn't meeting her needs. Add to that her own insecurity as a mom, and her personal mess grew worse and worse.

One day, when her children were still preschoolers, Julie looked in the mirror and felt as if she didn't recognize herself anymore. She used to be a confident woman with drive and dreams who could take on the world; now she was a mess who was always angry. "I finally realized I couldn't force having the relationship I wanted. I wanted *me* back. I honestly think my prayers even changed, from less of a 'God, just fix everything, and every*one*, around me' to 'Lord, just help me be better.'"

Julie gradually broke out of this cycle by owning her feelings. And it started with turning to God. She focused on the "joy" part of the happiness equation, which always comes first. It wasn't a question of doing an hour of devotions a day; she was too busy and that wasn't feasible. But she did intentionally bring God in on more aspects of her life. Instead of wallowing in self-doubt or running to the phone to ask a friend how to cope whenever she had anxiety, she'd pray. Those little prayers, peppered throughout her hectic day, gave her a different perspective. And that newly found spiritual intimacy with God brought the kind of joy that gradually lifted her out of her fog, showing her she wasn't alone and she didn't have to be responsible for her children's well-being and their future. God was carrying them too.

Action Step: Create "prayer cues" for your daily routine. Find times to regularly send up a prayer of thanksgiving or a prayer for help throughout your day. Suggestions: pray whenever you hear a siren, pull up to a stop sign, or do the dishes.

Once Julie involved God more in her everyday life, contentment came more readily. Now the focus of her day wasn't about being the perfect Christian wife and mom; it was about acting out of the personality and gifts that God had given her. She became more organized, which helped substantially, but she also accepted imperfection.

"I don't feel guilty anymore for saying, 'I don't have dinner made. What are we ordering?'" Julie reported. "Not making dinner every night does not make me a bad wife or mother."

Action Step: Get to know yourself better so that you know who God made you to be. Take the Myers-Briggs Type Indicator test, or the DISC personality test. Make a list of your strengths and then make a list of your weaknesses. Have a friend help, if necessary. Now look at your weaknesses and decide, "I will let myself off the hook for these things. I will not feel guilty that they are not my strengths. Nor will I feel guilty for not being someone else." Look at your strengths and ask, "How can I work in my strengths every day?"

She also realized that she was more than just a wife and a mom, so she intentionally added things to her life that brought her joy. She made a goal of biking all around her town and began taking bike rides that ranged from one to twelve miles a day whenever she could get a baby-sitter. She sat down and decided to finally write her novel. Even just these two things helped her to feel more contentment because she was tending to her needs for a creative outlet and a physical outlet.

And Julie discovered another element in being honest with herself. She did need help—just not from her husband. After talking to her doctor, she realized that she suffered from seasonal affective disorder, which triggered depression during the long winter days with no sunlight and no warmth. "If I have to take this teeny-tiny white pill and I feel normal and I'm not griping at my husband, why not do that?"

Action Step: Visit your doctor if you suspect you're suffering from depression, hormonal imbalances, or other ailments, such as anemia or hypothyroidism, that could affect your mood and your health.

Once Julie had rediscovered her joy and her contentment, happiness finally followed. Julie started to see that if she could take control of her emotions, stop expecting her husband to fix things, and start changing small things where she could, she wasn't just helping herself; she was giving her husband a gift too. He didn't feel inadequate anymore. He was able to enjoy the marriage again.

In a marriage, one person's unhappiness often causes both people to question whether the relationship is worth it. As Julie realized, "Why did I expect to have a healthy, happy *marriage* when at least one of us wasn't a healthy, happy *person*?"

PUTTING HAPPINESS IN ITS RIGHTFUL PLACE

Happiness isn't something your husband gives you; it's something you find yourself when you concentrate first on joy—by falling in love with God—and second on contentment—finding peace in your circumstances. That's what Shaunti Feldhahn found in her research of happy couples. In *The Surprising Secrets of Highly Happy Marriages,* she wrote, "Highly happy couples tend to put God at the center of their marriage and focus on Him, rather than on their marriage or spouse, for fulfillment and happiness."[7]

I spent the first few years of my marriage waiting for Keith to make me happy, which was largely why we were so miserable. Once we got our act together, though, and started thinking differently, we arrived at a "sweet spot." I knew Keith loved me, Keith knew I loved him, and we were able to laugh and play together again without all that tension. I remember one April night in 1996 when we were celebrating just how happy we were. We had a lovely one-year-old daughter—who was finally sleeping through the night—and we had just returned from the ultrasound, where we had learned that our second child was a boy.

But our happiness didn't last long. The next day the phone rang, and the doctor told me that something was wrong with the baby's heart.

Over the next months Keith and I clung to each other, almost in desperation, as we learned just how sick our little boy would be once he was born. And our fears proved true. We had twenty-nine wonderful days with our son, Christopher, on this earth before he passed away after heart surgery.

When we went in for the follow-up report, one of the physicians told us, "I should warn you that half of couples who face the death of a child divorce within a year." Now, I highly doubt the truth of that statistic, but there's no question that walking through horrible circumstances does put a strain on marriage. You're grieving, and you're angry, and you're so wrapped up in your feelings that it's hard to reach out and be kind to someone else.

If I had expected Keith to make me feel better, our marriage would have fallen apart. But I knew there was nothing Keith could do. My only chance for getting through my son's death with my heart intact wasn't to rely on my husband; it was to rely on God. So when I needed to yell, I yelled at God. When I needed to rage, I raged at God. And gradually my defenses broke down and I was able to absorb his perfect peace—a peace my husband could never have given me.

Our route to happiness doesn't go through our husbands; it comes through finding peace with the One who created and saved us. As Shaunti Feldhahn concluded, "Trusting God instead of another to meet your needs might be the most enduring security-producing choice you ever make."[8] I hope it's one you can make too.

Summary of Action Steps

1. Add a psalm or a song to start your day. Sing in the shower! Start the day saying thank you to God.

2. Whenever you share a frustration with your husband, be clear about what you want to get out of the conversation: Should he listen, fix it, or help you fix it?

3. Create prayer cues for your daily routine that will nudge you to talk with God throughout your day.

4. Take a personality inventory and a strengths inventory to figure out who you are. Let yourself off the hook for your weaknesses. Work more in your areas of strength.

5. Visit your doctor if you suspect your mood may have an underlying physical cause.

Thought #4

I Can't Mold My Husband into My Image

In my marriage, I wreck the cars. Keith wrecks the laundry, but that doesn't cost nearly as much. Keith recently backed into a tree and shattered our van's windshield, but since this was his one and only infraction in our whole relationship, we viewed it as an aberration rather than a pattern.

My husband and I have other differences too. Keith has the "all the lights in the house must be turned off if not needed" gene. I'm missing that one. His idea of a relaxing afternoon is to forge a new path through untrodden woods to look at birds; I like to knit. He likes war movies; I like Jane Austen. We're a strange pair.

As I told you earlier in the book, we started marriage with very different backgrounds and very different preferences. And yet, what often occurs to me now is how alike we've become.

I tend to be on the shy side. Today I make my living speaking at women's events, often in front of large groups, and this doesn't bother me whatsoever. But I find parties, where I have to talk one-on-one, uncomfortable. It's not natural for me to make small talk with strangers. It's not natural for Keith, on the other hand, to be quiet. And during our marriage, he has taken me to so many parties that I've begun to open up. But he's also started to quiet down. Had we not married, he might have been even more gregarious and I may have become more introverted.

Or take food. I crave sweets, but not fat or salt. Keith, on the other hand, once drank a cup of bacon grease because someone dared him. If Keith hadn't married me, he'd likely be a lot heavier than he is right now, and I'd probably still never know how wonderful real butter makes everything taste.

Over the last twenty-three years we have changed. I am not the same person who walked down that aisle, and he isn't the same one who was waiting for me. I loved him dearly then, but I love him much more deeply now. Just by being together, we change each other.

Thought #4: I can't mold my husband into my image.

Change for the better seems to be a key ingredient in many romances. Take the story of *Beauty and the Beast,* for instance. Belle sees great potential inside the Beast. Sure, everybody else is creeped out by him, but she knows that behind that ugly exterior is an upstanding, wonderful man who simply needs to be freed. And so she loves him, and because of her love, he has the courage to let the Real Him manifest. Her love changes him.

That's the story, isn't it?

Actually, it's not. The real *Beauty and the Beast* story goes more like this: At first Belle is pretty creeped out by the Beast. But as she gets to know him, she sees the Real Him. She admires and respects his character. And so she accepts and loves him—as a Beast. And because of that acceptance, he changes into the person he was meant to be. It's the acceptance that is the key to change.

Our husbands are not pieces of clay that we're supposed to mold into our own image. Our husbands have the right to be themselves—and when we accept that, our marriages tend to be much stronger.

MANIPULATING HIM TO CHANGE ALWAYS BACKFIRES

Okay, hold on a second. If change is inevitable in marriage, then doesn't that mean we *can* change our husbands?

Marriage is a living system that is always changing. But that kind of natural change is a two-way process that occurs as we adapt to each other. I didn't set out to be more gregarious at parties; I was hoping Keith would suddenly enjoy quiet nights at home. He didn't set out to enjoy chick flicks or travel. If we'd had the power to change the other in the direction we wanted, we wouldn't look the same as we do today. And we likely would not have grown nearly as much as individuals either.

Your husband will not stay the same person he was on your wedding day, but neither will you. While change is inevitable, it doesn't mean the change happens the way you plan. If you wait to accept your husband until he lives up to your expectations, you'll likely end up miserable. Ultimately the key to change in marriage is acceptance and intimacy and friendship, not coercion or rejection.

Yet that's hardly the message our culture gives us. Venture to your grocery store and check out the magazine covers, and you'll see headlines like "10 Ways to Make Your Man More Affectionate," "How to Get Your Husband to Do More Housework," and "How to Turn Your Husband into a Romance King." It's not about accepting him; it's about manipulating him so you can mold him into your own personal Ken doll.

Manipulation rarely gets us our desired results, because what we want is true intimacy: a meeting of two whole people who desire to be together and who love each other. If we're trying to change him, there can never be a meeting of two whole people. We're diminishing him and showing him we don't really love him for him. Acceptance, then, is a prerequisite for intimacy.

Does that mean that we accept all of his behavior? No, it doesn't, because accepting the person is different from accepting the behavior.

Sometimes we're told this:

Pat Answer: *Men need respect, so you must respect his decisions.*

That's not what I'm arguing. You don't necessarily respect his decisions; you respect and honor his *right* to make those decisions. You don't try to control him.

That may sound as though he has free license to do as he wants, and you're right—he does. But here's the catch: *so do you.* Just as he can choose, you can choose as well, and we'll look soon at how you can create a God-honoring marriage by choosing how you will respond if he does something hurtful. For now, though, put that on the back burner and realize, *My responsibility is not to change him but to accept him.*

Accepting the person looks like this:

Accept him as your husband: You choose to love him and stay committed to him. You won't let things he does that annoy you affect that commitment.

Accept him as a child of God: You accept that he is his own person who can make his own choices, and you honor his right to make choices—even if you don't agree with them. You aren't trying to control him.

KEEP MY EYES ON MYSELF—NOT ON HIM

The key to acceptance is to learn what my friend Julie did in the last chapter—we must take responsibility for our own stuff first, rather than expecting our husbands to make us happy.

Just a few years into her marriage, Becky Zerbe had a big wake-up call about her own responsibility to change her marriage. She had packed her bags, snatched up her fourteen-month-old child, and headed over to her parents' house, determined to leave her husband, Bill, behind. When she arrived, her mother calmly took out a piece of paper and drew a line down the middle. She asked Becky to write on the left-hand side of the paper a list of all the things Bill had done that had made her want to leave. Becky did so enthusiastically, sure that on the right-hand side her mom would ask her to write down Bill's good qualities. She wanted to make sure the left side would dwarf the right side.

But when Becky had finished writing down his bad qualities, her mom didn't ask her to list his good qualities. Instead, her mom instructed, "For each item on the left side, I want you to write how you responded." Becky was flabbergasted, but she wrote down all the petty things she had done. She had sulked. She had yelled. She had withdrawn and criticized. When she was finished, her mother tore the piece of paper in half and presented Becky with the list of her own failings. She told Becky to pray about those before she made any decisions.

Becky realized that she had been blaming Bill, but Bill was not the only one in the wrong. So she went home for good, and the things that once bugged her about him she began to find endearing.[1]

Blaming others is terribly counterproductive when it comes to growing a marriage. In their book *Boundaries in Marriage,* Drs. Henry Cloud and John Townsend wrote that instead of practicing blame, we need to start practicing ownership. Too often we say that our husbands "make us feel guilty" or "make us angry." We blame our behavior or our unhappiness on the other person.[2] And that makes us stuck, because if all our problems are someone else's fault, then there's nothing we can do to fix them.

Maybe what we need is a good dose of humility, just as God asks of us in Micah 6:8: we're to act justly, love mercy, and walk humbly with him. That humility helps us get our eyes off of what everyone else is doing wrong and back onto our own hearts. If we're always praying, "Change him!" while believing ourselves to be blameless, then it's hard to hear what God may be asking us to do. We haven't really humbled ourselves before him. Telling God, "I am yours. Change me," though, is often the starting point for real growth in a marriage. We're being honest with ourselves and honest with God, letting our defenses down so that we can hear more easily what God wants to say to us.

Before you get your back up, when I talk about asking God to change us, that doesn't only mean helping us to become kinder, as we talked about in Thought #1. Sometimes it's also asking God to do what might seem like the opposite—to help us become bolder; to help us "act justly" by standing up to injustice, even to our husbands. We don't dictate the way we change; God does. And he wants us to look more and more like Jesus in every way.

ACCEPTANCE INVOLVES RECOGNIZING OUR CHOICES

My inbox is flooded with e-mails from women who are frustrated with their husbands. Sometimes I read these e-mails with a rather large dose of confusion. Here's one example:

> Over the last six months, since our wedding, I've realized that my husband is a slob! He never cleans up anything. He's never affectionate—not even a peck on the cheek unless he wants sex. And he promised me he'd quit smoking, but he hasn't. And then he'll grab me and try to start something when he hasn't spoken to me all day, and I'll be like, "You stink like smoke," and he just gets mad. How do I get him to act like a man instead of a little boy?

They've been married for less than a year, and according to this wife, he does everything wrong. He smokes. He isn't affectionate. He's sly.

This new bride and many like her are terribly frustrated, and they're telling me these details so that I will commiserate with them. According to them, their husbands are idiots! But that's where my confusion comes in. I'm not sure what the benefit is of having other people agree that your husband is an idiot, because you were the one who chose him. If he's a complete idiot, what does that say about your ability to make good choices?

My oldest daughter is engaged to a guy at her university who shares a house with four other young men from their InterVarsity Christian Fellowship (IVCF) group. One day three of these guys acted out a Jedi fight—complete with towels on heads and sound effects—while their three girlfriends sat on the couch, watching in incredulity. When one girl dared to protest, "You guys are too weird," the three guys stopped and said simultaneously, "Hey, you chose this."

And the boys had a point.

Action Step: Remind yourself why you chose him. Write a list of at least six qualities your husband has that drew you to him. Write down two specific things he did that helped you to know you loved him. Keep that list by your bed, and every night write down one thing your husband did that day that showed a quality you had already listed. Thank God for that specific quality in your husband.

We choose these creatures to marry—silly creatures who take risks and find blowing things up mesmerizing and body noises humorous. And yet somehow, once we're married, this tendency to be silly or dangerous starts to grate on us when dishes need to be done or big decisions need to be made or a baby needs diapers changed. And so we try to change him, in hopes that he will become less impulsive and risky and wild and more like us.

Is that really what you want? After all, those differences—those very manly things—attracted you to him in the first place. The root of many marriage problems is a failure to accept that this person is the man you chose to marry and that your marriage vows mean something.

Acceptance Brings Contentment

My blogging friend Cheri laughs about how naive she was before she married. "I still have a letter I sent home when we were dating, in which I told my parents he was the male version of me." Yet she couldn't have been more wrong. Once they married, she soon realized he wasn't just "a best friend you had sex with." He was actually more like Spock, or, in more modern media language, Sheldon from *The Big Bang Theory*. Though undiagnosed at the time, her husband had Asperger's. He was brilliant and fascinating, but he had little understanding of most human emotions.

Right after their honeymoon, the two of them were arranging their furniture in the married student housing complex, and they could not agree about where to put the couch. Cheri had definite opinions, but her husband had logic on his side.

"A friend would have said, 'Whatever you want is fine,' but my husband didn't like to lose an argument. He went to the mat for the couch," she said.

That was the first in a long line of arguments that her husband won over the next decade because he was so logical that she couldn't refute him. Instead, she'd often burst into tears.

"To a girlfriend, this would have been the signal to come closer," Cheri explained. But her husband's family dismissed people who would cry. And so they grew further apart.

Soon Cheri found herself showing contempt, the prime predictor of divorce, according to marriage researcher John Gottman.[3] She nagged, she questioned his judgment, and she emasculated him. She saw herself as superior because she understood emotions and he didn't. When he did something she didn't like, she'd roll her eyes. She'd use a condescending tone of voice. If he mispronounced a word, she'd jump on it, just so she could show him up. And their children started following her lead.

"I was treating him worse than I would a stranger," Cheri admitted sadly.

Finally she packed her bags, but she stuck them in the closet. She decided she wouldn't actually leave until the next big blowout, so she could blame him for forcing her out.

In the interim, though, she experienced a turning point. Cheri realized she hadn't tried a whole lot of anything to fix the marriage except blaming him for being the way he was. She had been sad, and she had been lonely, and she had cried—but she had never actually done anything to mend the rift.

So she gave God a year to change things. She was still hoping that God would take the lead and change her husband, but over the course of that year she started to be open to what she needed to work on too. She realized much of the problem was her own expectations, her own attitude, and her own behavior. She was rehashing every hurt and blowing it out of proportion.

Cheri went through the complaint-free challenge we talked about in Thought #2.[4] But the biggest breakthrough came at a spiritual retreat. "As the weekend progressed, I realized that I had been asking my husband to rescue me from myself, and I had put him in the place where only God can be." She was asking for something her husband, a flawed human being, could not give. And so Cheri decided to run to God instead. "You know," Cheri admitted with a laugh, "if we had been more compatible, I'd have no need for God."

Action Step: Turn contempt into acceptance. For a week, make a conscious effort to take a breath before you react to your husband. Allow that breathing time to help you stop eye rolling, control your tone of voice, and halt any attempt to correct him.

Cheri told me about the distance in her marriage and the fights and even her past sexual refusal. And yet as she told me her story, our Skype conversation was interrupted throughout by banter between her and her husband, who was in another room. When he had to run an errand, Cheri threw off the head-phones and said to me with a sly smile, "I'll be right back! I've got to go kiss him before he leaves." This woman, who had wrestled with God about the lack of love with her Spock husband, was giggling like a schoolgirl about this man who now held her heart.

She had accepted him. She had stopped trying to change him—and thus had stopped showing contempt for him. And she let God meet her needs. In the end, they found that fun relationship she had always yearned for.

If It Does Depend on Me, I Have to Do Something

Acceptance frees both my husband and me—but it is only the first step. In Romans 12:18, Paul wrote, "If it is possible, as far as it depends on you, live at peace with everyone." We are to be responsible for what is in our control, while also recognizing that not everything is. Everybody has the ability and the right to make their own choices, even bad ones. Sometimes those we love will make poor choices. But that does not absolve us of the responsibility to do what *is* in our control.

In the last chapter we talked about how we shouldn't rely on our husbands for our happiness, and that's true. But here I want to go a little further. It's not *only* that we shouldn't wait for our husbands to change or that we shouldn't expect them to meet all our needs. It's that we need to take the initiative to make changes ourselves.

Right now there's a balance in your relationship. It may be an unhealthy one, but you are in balance. You each do certain things, and that has become your normal.

What if you don't like normal?

Relationships naturally find their own resting place. Like a teeter-totter, they come to rest where you each play your role. That resting place isn't necessarily healthy. He may be taking all the weight of the teeter-totter by being too controlling, or you may be taking not enough weight by being too timid. But there are two ways to change that balance of a teeter-totter: either you move or he moves. When one of you moves, that teeter-totter will shift and find a new balance. That's how you end up changing each other! You don't need to try to change your husband; you simply change yourself, and that creates a new "normal" in your relationship. So let's look at four ways we can change the dynamic in our marriage—not by trying to change our husbands, but simply by changing ourselves.

1. Ask for What I Want

Everyone has expectations going into marriage, but rarely do we realize these are expectations. We figure they're facts: "This is just the way the world works." We forget that his world may have been different from our world, and thus he may not have the same assumptions about life. When he doesn't put his laundry in the hamper, we often interpret it as a personal slight and think, *He expects me to pick up his stuff.* Perhaps he just doesn't particularly care about dirty clothes being on the floor, doesn't notice when they're there, and doesn't realize that it's bugging you.

Doesn't realize it's bugging me? How could he be that obtuse?

In *The Good News About Marriage,* Shaunti Feldhahn shared the statistic that in 82 percent of marriages in which at least one spouse is unhappy, the other spouse doesn't know there's anything wrong.[5] You may be seething inside and you may be hurt, but your spouse may not even realize it.

Some of my readers recently shared stories on my Facebook page about asking their husbands for help. Lynn said,

> Early in our marriage, I hinted several times that it would be nice if the clean dishes got put away. Finally I got mad at my husband and we argued about it. He told me, "Just tell me what you want me to do, and I'll do it." I thought it was too rude to order him around, but that's the way he wanted. Then we were visiting his mom, and she was hinting at something he should do. When she left the room, I told him, "Your mom wants you to do this." He balked and said, "No way. I lived with my mom much longer than you, and I'd know." When she came back, he asked her straight out and she said, "Yes, of course. What took you so long?"

I thought it was too rude to order him around. We often don't ask because we fear it's demeaning, and yet most men would far rather be asked than hinted at. In asking directly we treat our husbands like grown-ups. They can choose to refuse, but at least they know what we want. Hinting is like asking them to read minds, which is disrespectful.

That idea of having to ask for help, though, grated on my reader Lindsey. "I shouldn't have to ask!" she told herself. "He can *see* the mess!" Then one day during an argument, her husband grew quiet and said, "Baby, I just don't see the mess the way you do. I'm just not as good as you are at juggling the house, chores, and bills. I don't multitask like you do. I'm sorry." Ever since then, Lindsey has learned to ask—and not to ask for a thousand things at once either!

Both Lynn and Lindsey wasted so much emotional energy seething because their husbands weren't taking care of what they considered basic responsibilities. Yet when asked for help, their husbands were actually more than willing to comply.

Action Step: Pick one thing that is bugging you and ask your husband to help you in this area this week.

2. Pursue Things That Bring Me Happiness

Unfortunately, asking for help doesn't work in every marriage. My friend Jeannie tried asking her corporate executive husband to stay home for more family time, but he refused. He loved her, he loved the kids, but his job took precedence. She was angry and sad and worried that the kids would grow up without knowing him. They never had any fun as a family. They just stayed around the house, hoping that Daddy would walk in the door in time for dinner.

Finally Jeannie realized she faced a choice. She could accept the fact that her husband would always work long hours, or she could grow bitter and make the kids miserable in the process. She decided acceptance was the better route. But it didn't end there.

She had dreams of trips she wanted to take with the kids—camping and Disneyland and even picnics in the park on a Sunday afternoon. She had put all of these dreams on hold, thinking that it wasn't right to do them without her husband. But she decided that if these things would make her happy, she should do them anyway and stop waiting for her husband to bring her that happiness.

As she started to plan fun things for her and the children, she also began to notice that her husband made more of an effort to be home for some of them. Home wasn't stressful for him in the same way, because he didn't feel condemnation when he stepped in the door. Yet even if he hadn't come home more, she still would have been happier. And that happiness brought a lightness to her marriage. Her husband didn't feel responsible for fixing things in the same way, and that gave him more freedom to join them guilt-free.

If there is something you desperately want that your husband doesn't seem to share, add it anyway. Doing so is part of creating the happiness that benefits everyone, and it relieves your husband of the obligation to fix your dissatisfaction.

Action Step: Include some life-giving things in your life. Pick one thing that you've been putting off doing and schedule it in.

3. Quit Overfunctioning

Geri Scazzero, author of *The Emotionally Healthy Woman,* was a mom of four with far too much on her plate. Her idea of a Perfect Christian Wife was someone who had it all under control. Her house was perfect; her kids were her center; and if anyone from church ever needed anything, she dropped everything to help.

Geri's husband was an inner-city pastor committed to outreach. Frequently, on a whim, he would invite others to the house for a meal, and Geri would have to figure out how to throw something together for a crowd and then still get the kids' homework done and drive them to their activities.

One day she couldn't take it anymore. She resented that she was always so busy while her family seemed to have an easy life. And she realized that they wouldn't ever start functioning until *she* stopped doing everything for them. Geri explained, "We overfunction when we do for others what they can and should do for themselves. Overfunctioners prevent people, including themselves, from growing up. . . . Wherever you find an overfunctioner, an underfunctioner inevitably follows close behind."[6]

Geri realized that she was becoming a person she didn't like. She was bitter. She was sarcastic. She complained a lot. In the process, by doing so much, she was helping others in the family become people she didn't like either. They took her for granted. They showed ingratitude. They weren't responsible. Chief among these was her husband. And finally it hit her: "If I wanted Pete to stop underfunctioning at home, I needed to stop overfunctioning."[7] She didn't try to control Pete or tell him what to do. She simply put limits on herself, deciding what she would do and what she would no longer do. Then others had the choice of how they would respond. The Scazzeros became a more peaceful, more functional, and less chaotic family when Geri started saying no.

> **Action Step:** Quit overfunctioning. If you're doing things for your family they should do for themselves, start retreating to leave a void they can fill.

4. Allow Others to Reap What They Sow

Adeline was a busy homeschool mom of six kids. She loved God, volunteered at children's church, and mentored young wives. She felt valued everywhere—except in her marriage, where she felt constantly belittled and hurt by her husband, Cole, who would yell, criticize, and say cruel and crude things without ever apologizing. For twenty years Adeline read books on how to be a better wife, listened to sermons on forgiveness and having a gentle spirit, and prayed unceasingly for God to make her a peaceful and loving partner who wouldn't cause such strife.

Adeline had accepted the blame for the problems in the relationship, and had been in agony trying to solve them. Meanwhile, Cole could say what he wanted and do what he wanted, while his family catered to him.

Part of living out God's purpose, according to Micah 6:8, is to "act justly." That means pursuing justice within our relationships. In Galatians 6:7, Paul expanded on God's plan for justice: "Do not be deceived: God cannot be mocked. A man reaps what he sows." In *Boundaries in Marriage,* Drs. Henry Cloud and John Townsend named this "the Law of Sowing and Reaping." We are supposed to bear the consequences for our actions. In Adeline's case, though, Cole was sowing discord, selfishness, and cruelty, and Adeline and her kids were reaping the consequences. Adeline was disrupting the law of sowing and reaping by taking away one of the best tools God has for molding Cole into God's image.

As Adeline's children became teenagers, they started to see the family dynamic more clearly, and they sat their mother down and told her that Cole was being mean, unreasonable, and unchristian. At the same time as the children came to notice the behavior, Adeline finally realized that she could not be nice enough or sweet enough to change an unreasonable person. This passage from John Townsend's book *Who's Pushing Your Buttons?* stood out to her especially:

> I have seen the law of sowing and reaping work in powerful ways when people allowed the button-pusher to experience it. Conversely, I have seen it interrupted by well-meaning rescuers and enablers, and its power gets temporarily nullified by those willing to help the person avoid the consequences. God chastises those whom he loves (Hebrews 12:6). Do not make the mistake of getting between your difficult person and God's rules.[8]

Adeline decided to start letting the law of sowing and reaping take effect in her marriage. If her husband criticized or spoke cruelly to her, she would remove herself from the room, saying, "I won't listen to you while you speak like that." She told him that she could not be physically intimate with him when he was cruel without repentance.

Action Step: Allow others to reap what they sow. Respect their right to make choices, but draw a clear boundary that says, "When you do this, I will also choose to do this."

If you are in a marriage like Adeline's, please understand that it isn't God's best that your husband disparage you. What's best is if both spouses learn to truly love each other intimately. So if you are committed to loving your husband, committed to honoring the marriage, and committed to seeing that marriage become healthy, you have to make some changes. *Whatever you tolerate will continue.* If he's doing something wrong, not just something that's irritating, you need to stop tolerating it.

This is not the same as trying to change him. It simply means that you change *how you react to him.* As Drs. Cloud and Townsend said, responding in this way gives husbands like Cole an opportunity to reap the loneliness they've been sowing—and gives them impetus to treat family members with more kindness.

But here's the other lesson: even if he doesn't change, you have still made life better for yourself. You are removing yourself from a painful situation, while still respecting your husband. You're telling him, "You have the right to be angry, but I also have the right not to listen when you yell." You accept him as a child of God who can make choices, but you realize that you also are a child of God with the ability to choose. That's what Adeline did, and she's finding that after years of trying to win her husband's favor, she can finally experience and feel God's favor.

Your husband is not a piece of clay for you to mold; but *you* are a piece of clay that God wants to mold. Isaiah 64:8 says, "Yet you, LORD, are our Father. We are the clay, you are the potter; we are all the work of your hand." As we accept our husbands, God will start changing us—and that may involve learning to stand up to bad behavior, as Adeline did, or it may involve accepting our own responsibility for making the marriage difficult, as Becky did. But the only one capable of truly changing anyone is God. Let's not try to do God's job. Let's lean into God and let him do his work in us.

Summary of Action Steps

1. Remind yourself why you chose your husband. Make a list of all the qualities that attracted you to him.

2. Turn contempt into acceptance. Take a breath before you react to your husband. Allow that breathing time to help you stop eye rolling, control your tone of voice, and halt any attempt to correct him.

3. Pick one thing that is bugging you and ask your husband to help you in this area this week.

4. Include some joy in your life. Pick one thing that you've been putting off doing and schedule it in.

5. Quit overfunctioning. If you're doing things for your family they should do for themselves, start retreating to leave a void they can fill.

6. Allow others to reap what they sow. Respect their right to make choices, but draw a clear boundary that says, "When you do this, I will also choose to do this."

Thought #5

I'm Not in Competition with My Husband

've never consciously submitted to my husband. I have chosen not to do something I've wanted to do so that I could make his life easier. I have thought of his favorite food when deciding what to make for dinner. I've taken it to heart when he's told me I'm coddling one of the girls, and I've made my schedule lighter when he worried I was burning myself out. But I've never thought in terms of "submitting." I've simply thought, *This is my husband, and I love him, and I want to please him.*

I suppose that's what submission boils down to, but I usually recoil at the word. It's often been used in Christian circles in a way that seems to suggest that husbands should be sergeant majors and wives should be lowly privates ready and eager to obey. That doesn't sound like an intimate marriage; that sounds like a power trip.

I don't think submission was ever supposed to mean that, so let's look at how it entered our marriage lexicon in the first place to see if we can flesh out its real intention. In Ephesians 5:21, Paul admonishes us, "Submit to one another out of reverence for Christ." Mutual submission, then, is a hallmark of the Christian life, a natural outpouring of "[walking] humbly with your God" (Micah 6:8). Paul then went on to explain what submission will look like to specific groups of people:

> Wives, submit yourselves to your own husbands as you do to the Lord. For the husband is the head of the wife as Christ is the head of the church, his body, of which he is the Savior. Now as the church submits to Christ, so also wives should submit to their husbands in everything.
>
> Husbands, love your wives, just as Christ loved the church and gave himself up for her to make her holy, cleansing her by the washing with water through the word, and to present her to himself as a radiant church, without stain or wrinkle or any other blemish, but holy and blameless. In this same way, husbands ought to love their wives as their own bodies. He who loves his wife loves himself. After all, no one ever hated their own body, but they feed and care for their body, just as Christ does the church—for we are members of his body. "For this reason a man will leave his father and mother and be united to his wife, and the two will become one flesh." This is a profound mystery—but I am talking about Christ and the church. However, each one of you also must love his wife as he loves himself, and the wife must respect her husband. (Ephesians 5:22–33)

At marriage conferences, when I ask what people think the word *submission* means, inevitably women hem and haw until they finally conclude something like, "If we disagree on something, he gets the final say." That lines up well with our pat answer, which states:

> **Pat Answer:** *The husband is the authority in the family. In a disagreement, he decides, and she obeys. When you do this, the family will experience God's blessing.*

Does that strike you as odd? God put all those words in the Bible simply to say, "In the case of ties, husbands win"?

When it comes to submission, I think the immortal words from *The Princess Bride* sum up our experience well: "You keep using that word. I do not think it means what you think it means."[1] So let's look first at what submission is not, and then we'll get a better picture of what submission is.

SUBMISSION IS NOT PRIMARILY ABOUT WHO IS IN CHARGE

The original Greek word for *submission* suggests the idea of placing yourself "under" someone. This isn't an authoritarian position—although it's not surprising that we tend to think of it as hierarchical. After all, what do you picture when you read the phrase "the husband is the head of the wife," as Paul wrote in Ephesians 5:23? If you're like most modern English speakers, you think of Bill Gates acting as head of Microsoft: he's the head honcho, the one who makes the decisions, the one who is in charge. Or you picture a sergeant in an army, commanding the men in his unit to "go take that hill!" *Head,* to us in English, means being the boss.

There's a Greek word that means the exact same thing—a Greek word that means "head of an army" or "head of an enterprise." That Greek word is *archon.* There's only one problem. That's not the Greek word for "head" that Paul used here. Instead, Paul deliberately used the word *kephale,* which is more like "source," as in the head of a river. That's more in line with the rest of that sentence, which says, "the husband is the head of the wife *as Christ is the head of the church, his body, of which he is the Savior.*" How does Christ live out his headship? Paul tells us that he "gave himself up for her [the church]" (verse 25). He didn't bark orders; he lovingly sacrificed himself for the church, and Paul asks husbands to do the same for their wives.[2]

Head as "source" rather than "boss" gives more of a sense of taking the initiative, just as Jesus took the initiative to save his church. Even biologically that makes sense. Men were created to be the primary sexual initiators, and women the primary responders. (This doesn't mean that women can't initiate sex! Only that women were created to be on the receiving end.)

My friends Derek and Lisa show this initiator/responder relationship well. For the last twenty years Derek has worked hard to lead his family spiritually. They pray before meals, they go to church every Sunday, and Derek listens to sermons on Christian radio stations as he works. But last summer he had the chance to go on a mission trip to El Salvador with their teenage son.

That trip stirred something in Derek. A few weeks ago we sat across the table at a restaurant as Derek explained the impact it had on him to take dozens of orphans to a day at the beach and, later in the week, to help them build new homes. He's on fire like I've never seen him before. And Lisa was sitting next to him, smiling quietly. Lisa doesn't feel quite the same pull, but she sees the change in Derek. So when he asked her to arrange to take a three-week leave of absence so they could go back together—Derek wanted to experience it with his wife—she agreed. Not because Derek is in authority, but because God was leading him somewhere and Lisa wanted to be a part of that.

Thought #5:

I'm not in competition with my husband.

Action Step: Ask yourself, *Where is God leading my husband right now? What are two specific ways I can support him in this?* (Prayer, volunteering with him, researching something, et cetera.)

Treating marriage like a hierarchical relationship makes it sound as though wives and husbands are constantly at odds and someone needs to have the final say. It indicates that we're in competition, not in unity. I think this is the wrong way to look at it.

We're not on opposite teams; we're on the same team!

SUBMISSION DOESN'T MEAN I BLINDLY OBEY

Unfortunately, instead of understanding this teamwork dynamic, we often see submission in terms of obedience. I was discussing this idea recently with my friend and fellow marriage conference speaker Sharol. Using the "obey your husband" definition of submission, she realized that in her whole four-decades-long marriage, she had submitted only once. On that occasion, her husband felt called to a particular ministry that required relocating to another city. She didn't feel that calling, but she knew it was important to him, so she decided to follow. Within a few months she felt the calling too. Just like Lisa and Derek, he initiated, and Sharol responded.

Usually in the marriage, though, when Sharol and her husband don't agree, they work through it until they do. And they've tackled big issues: whether she would quit her full-time job; who should be the stay-at-home parent; whether to pursue a pastoring opportunity. They wanted to agree, so they wrestled together until they did.

I don't understand why some women take pride in saying, "I let him make all the decisions, even if I think he's wrong." If you think your husband is wrong, you have an issue in your relationship. A disagreement by definition means that one of you—or both of you—is not listening to God. Wouldn't it be better, and more in line with Scripture, to do as Sharol and her husband, Neil, do: wrestle it through together, pray fervently together and individually, and seek counsel until you're on the same page? If you're always deferring to your husband without wrestling and talking things through, then you could easily prevent oneness, not enhance it.

But wait, you may be saying, How can submission *not* be about decisions and obedience, when Ephesians 5:24 says that women should submit to their husbands "in everything"? Then there's 1 Peter 3:5–6, which says, "This is the way the holy women of the past who put their hope in God used to make themselves beautiful. They were submissive to their own husbands, like Sarah, who obeyed Abraham and called him her master. You are her daughters if you do what is right and do not give way to fear" (NIV, 1984).

Sarah obeyed Abraham and called him master. That means we should obey our husbands too, doesn't it?

On my blog I was recently talking about what to do if a husband is making poor financial decisions. If he wants to lie on a loan application, and he asks the wife to cosign that loan, what should she do? One commenter replied, "She has to obey her husband, even if he's wrong. If she refuses to sign, she is disobeying God. And she'll incur judgment from God for that. She is to obey her husband as her lord."

Hold on a second. Does Scripture really say that we are to obey our husbands, even if they're wrong? Most of my Facebook commenters seemed to think so. When I asked what submission meant to them, the vast majority gave a definition pertaining to obedience: "You're to obey your husband just as you obey God or a military commander."

Is that really what Peter meant? In Acts 5, Luke records the story of husband and wife Ananias and Sapphira. They were early disciples who wanted to win brownie points with their fellow Christians. So they sold a piece of property, and then Ananias brought a portion of the money—not the whole sale price—and gave it to the disciples, claiming that amount was all he received. After Peter reprimanded him for his deception, Ananias was struck dead.

A little while later Sapphira walked in and Peter asked her, "Is this the price you received for the property?" She replied that it was, and then Peter said, "How is it that you have *agreed together* to put the Spirit of the Lord to the test? Look, the feet of those who have buried your husband are at the door, and they will carry you out" (Acts 5:9, NRSV). Sapphira was then struck dead too.

Peter told Sapphira that it would have been better for her to have gone her own way than to agree with her husband to lie. Let's remember: Peter was the one who encouraged wives to obey husbands as Sarah obeyed Abraham and called him her master. Yet Peter was also the same apostle who made it clear that you should never obey your husband if he leads you into sin.

In fact, Peter would have been the last person to say that we should ever put a human authority in God's place! Later in the same chapter of Acts, Peter and the other apostles were arrested by the Sanhedrin (the council of Jewish leaders) and imprisoned for preaching about Jesus. During the night, an angel appeared to them and freed them from jail, so they began to preach again. When the Jewish leaders saw this, they were perturbed, to say the least. So they had Peter and the apostles brought before them, and told them in no uncertain terms that they were to shut their mouths about Jesus. Then Luke recorded in Acts 5:29, "Peter and the other apostles replied: 'We must obey God rather than human beings!'" No human authority is ever to be given supremacy over God—and that includes your husband.

Sapphira was punished for obeying her husband, and in the Old Testament, Abigail is praised and rewarded for disobeying her husband. In 1 Samuel 25 you can read her story. She was married to an absolute lout named Nabal. When David, before he was king, asked Nabal for supplies in return for the protection he had provided for Nabal's herds and servants, Nabal turned him away. Abigail knew that this meant certain death to them and to their servants, so she went up to David and intervened. David spared her and their servants, though God soon struck Nabal down. And David commended Abigail and married her. She didn't submit and follow Nabal blindly. She actually went behind his back and did what Peter told Sapphira she ought to have done: she asked, "What does God want me to do in this situation?"

God does not ask women to blindly obey their husbands. We are supposed to "act justly and to love mercy and to walk humbly with your God" (Micah 6:8), and that applies to marriage too. We are to walk humbly with God, not follow our husbands away from him. If following our husbands means going against God's commands, we're to follow God instead.

SUBMISSION DOESN'T MEAN I'M LESS THAN MY HUSBAND

A closer look at Scripture also dispels the idea that women are supposed to give up their own thoughts or opinions in marriage. For instance, when God created Eve, he called her a "help meet" for Adam (Genesis 2:18, KJV). Some have written that this means a woman's purpose is only to be fulfilled in relation to her husband, which is shoddy theology.[3] We are all made in God's image, and women are made in that image just as much as men are. If a woman's only role is to support a husband's pursuits, then what happens to single women, or to widows, or even to children? Do they not have a role in God's kingdom?

Writer Carolyn Custis James was wrestling with whether God's plan for women was too small when she started an investigation into what the word "help meet"—or *ezer* in Hebrew—actually meant. She discovered it's used sixteen times in the Old Testament in reference to God, so it can't have any connotation of subordination. And to her surprise, it usually has a strong military connotation, as in Deuteronomy 33:29: "Blessed are you, Israel! Who is like you, a people saved by the LORD? He is your shield and helper [*ezer*] and your glorious sword." She wrote, "Based on the Old Testament's consistent usage of this term, it only makes sense to conclude that God created the woman to be a warrior."[4] We're not weak; we're strong! And we help our husbands out of that strength, not as a person of lesser importance.

In *Fully Alive,* Larry Crabb explored this idea in great detail and similarly concluded that the phrase "help meet suitable for him" actually empowers women. We were made specifically to be suitable to stand with our husbands and be the partners they need.

Unfortunately, Larry himself didn't always understand this. In his book, he recounted how upon his nuptials, he expected that he would make the decisions in his marriage; he would lead and his wife would follow. "I saw myself as a friendly but firm sergeant looking at a female private who, for her own good, was required to do what I said."[5] At first it felt like a heady rush for him. But then the responsibility began to weigh heavily.

"Like a surgeon directing a nurse as they perform open-heart surgery, I had to get it right. Like the nurse, my wife's job was to follow my lead, no questions asked and advice given only on request. And like the surgeon, my responsibility was to make no mistakes."[6] As he began to doubt his ability to lead his wife perfectly, stirrings began in his heart that he desired a partner, not a servant. And a partner is more what God had in mind, for the word *suitable* means that she is capable of helping him—for whatever he must deal with in this life.

Proverbs 27:17 tells us, "As iron sharpens iron, so one person sharpens another." Unfortunately, too many of us are not acting as iron in our marriages. We are acting more like rags, helpful for polishing a sword, but not helpful for actually making that sword effective. That isn't the route to godliness; that's the route to a very unhealthy dynamic.

Carmen, one of my blog readers, worked as head of human resources in a large corporation. All day she managed people, their emotions, and their productivity. At home, though, she felt that she should let her husband navigate their complicated relationships with three preteens and teenagers. She did little as she watched her kids become social media junkies and leave messes in their wake. Her husband believed in a more laissez-faire form of parenting. He rarely demanded anything of their children and didn't back up Carmen if she suggested it was chore time.

She prayed about it and struggled with it, as she admitted, "I started not to like the people my kids were becoming. They were lazy and often talked back, and yet my husband kept saying it was just a phase."

The tipping point came when she found her sixteen-year-old son had downloaded porn onto his computer. She decided that leaving things to her husband wasn't working. Instead, she sat her husband down and asked him, "Can we set goals and responsibilities for the kids, and start doing more family things together?" Because he was devastated by the porn use too, he relented.

Carmen drew up a list of house rules, which included eating dinner together as a family, doing weekly chores, and having to earn time on their computers. She set up a Wi-Fi password and changed it daily. "The kids resisted at first, but we ended up much closer. We became a family again rather than five separate people doing their own thing." However, Carmen still mourns her oldest son, who has turned from God. She wonders if things would have been different if she had stepped up earlier.

Carmen and her husband learned an important lesson: Carmen is better at goal setting and motivating people than her husband is. Her unique giftings can be a "help" to her husband as they parent together. By holding back, she didn't act as a help meet; she instead created an environment where her husband could ignore some of his parenting responsibilities. Saying nothing when she knew something was wrong didn't promote godliness— for her or for anyone else in the house.

Action Step: Sit down with your husband and make a list of what "skills" go into running your household and your family. Then ask: Who is gifted at what? Who enjoys what? Are there areas where you can help each other more?

We often pay lip service to the idea that God designed marriage primarily to make us holy and not only to make us happy,[7] but then we seem to forget that this applies to men too. What if you are the vehicle through which God wants to grow and stretch your husband?

Deferring to Your Husband Is Not the Answer to Every Marriage Problem

I think many of the slanted views on submission come because there are only a few places in Scripture where wives are specifically told what to do in marriage, and two of them—Ephesians 5 and 1 Peter 3—pertain to submission.[8] Whenever a marriage problem pops up then, the thinking goes, obeying your husband must be the answer!

Many women struggle with passive husbands who play video games for hours on end, and in one particular blog post I brainstormed practical solutions that did not involve either manipulating or demeaning a husband. Several commenters, though, chimed in, saying, "Ultimately he is the head. If he chooses to play video games, you need to respect that and submit to his decisions." If we do that, they believe, he'll start taking leadership.

Pat Answer: *If your husband isn't stepping up to the plate and being a leader, it's because you're not submitting. If you step back, he will become a leader.*

That approach assumes that the reason your husband is playing video games so much is because of how you are acting. You are usurping control in the marriage, so he is emasculated and is retreating. However, I can think of many other reasons why he may be obsessed with his Xbox. He may have a longstanding addiction. He may not have been affirmed in his manhood by his dad growing up, and so he has trouble taking initiative. He may be depressed. If you step back and "submit," are you being a "suitable helper" to him? Or are you enabling him?

I recently read the story of a woman who was married for fifty years to an alcoholic. It was a difficult marriage, filled with his rages and very little affection. Their children did not fare well. But this woman praised God for giving her the strength to keep their family under one roof, submit to her husband, and let him be the head.

It made me sad, because I kept wondering, *What if God wanted to use the consequences of his actions to help motivate him to quit drinking?* She was allowing him to escape the consequences by fixing the problems he was causing. Just as we read Adeline's story about setting boundaries in Thought #4, sometimes we need to let our spouses reap what they sow. It is wonderful that this older woman learned patience, grace, and reliance on God. But it seems as if her family paid a large price.

> **Action Step:** If you worry that you are enabling a particular sin or bad habit of your husband's, choose one of the books on boundaries in marriage listed in the appendix and read through it prayerfully to see if you need to make some changes.

SUBMISSION IS ABOUT ONENESS

Part of the problem with viewing submission through the decision-making lens is that we make submission too *small*. Christianity is about servanthood and living out God's purposes in our daily lives. Shouldn't submission be about that too—something we do daily, not once every forty years, as my friend Sharol did?

In most marriage ceremonies, Genesis 2:24 is read aloud: "That is why a man leaves his father and mother and is united to his wife, and they become one flesh." God's desire for us isn't a tug-of-war relationship where one person gets his way; it's for true oneness! And I think that submission—"putting ourselves under" our husbands and willingly pursuing our husband's best—is the primary tool to attain this oneness. In humility, we become willing to think of his needs, his wants, his interests, his desires, before we think of our own. We pursue his best before we pursue our best. I think that's a taller order than just "in the event of ties, he wins." We don't just defer to him. We emotionally and physically invest in building him up and pursuing his best. And that sounds much more like the nature of the gospel to me. We serve. We love. We show grace. And our husbands serve us too, as they love us as Christ loved the church—even as they love their own bodies.

We've been looking at Micah 6:8 as an overarching verse for marriage—about acting justly and loving mercy. But the latter part of the verse is crucial too: we walk humbly with our God. That humility is the key to submission. Humility says, *I won't pursue only my own needs; I want to look to yours as well.*

In the first few years of my marriage, I wasn't submitting because I was focused almost entirely on my own pain. Eventually I realized I needed to make a change and start reaching out to my husband. But changing the way we think is hard. It took practice. Every day as I was walking home from my university classes and preparing to see my husband, I had to force myself to think, *How can I support Keith tonight? What does he need from me? Can I make dinner by myself so he can study? Can I do some errands for him?* And, of course, there was always, *Can I start getting in the mood now?*

I didn't want to think these things. I wanted to get home and collapse and read a book. But I had to train myself that when I walked through the door, the first thing I thought of was Keith.

Doors have become my "put Keith first signal" in our marriage. I used to talk myself into thinking of Keith first as I was walking home; these days, I'm usually the one at home and Keith's the one who walks through that door. But I listen for his keys, and as long as I don't have a pot boiling over, I rush to the door and give him a kiss. I ask him how his day was. I focus on him. And I make sure that when he does arrive home, even if he's late, or even if I've had a bad day, that those first few moments are about

him, not about me. It's a daily practice of putting his needs ahead
of my own.

Action Step: Today, find one specific, practical way that you
can "put yourself under" your husband. Maybe it's spending time
with him instead of on housework; maybe it's cooking his favorite
meal; maybe it's watching a game with him. Train yourself to
think, *How can I care practically for my husband today?*

BUT WHAT ABOUT MY HUSBAND
BEING THE SPIRITUAL LEADER?

I can't leave a chapter on submission without addressing the spiritual leader conundrum. A reader e-mailed me this question:

> I love my husband. He is a good man, father, and pro-
> vider. But he is *not* a spiritual leader. We've been married
> five years. I've prayed the entire time that he would step
> up. He goes to church with me and brings up something
> in the Bible maybe twice a year. I've tried to talk to him
> about it (he always goes on the defense and then declares
> himself a failure). I've tried nudging him in the right
> direction. I've tried leaving it alone and just praying. I
> don't feel right taking his place in leading our family
> (kids). I sometimes don't even want to grow in my walk
> because I don't want to be the "stronger" Christian. I'm
> worn and I'm broken. How do I inspire him to lead?

Nothing replaces knowing God's Word, and praying together as a couple definitely binds you together. Nevertheless, sometimes our expectations around what this will look like actually drive us apart—and then we do the opposite of submitting! Instead of walking humbly, we start to judge harshly.

> **Pat Answer:** *If you want to stay close together, you must do devotions together as a couple and as a family. He needs to step up and be the spiritual leader so that you pray together and read your Bible together, or you'll never feel close.*

That's what my reader seems to expect, but she's allowing that expectation to drive a wedge between her and her husband.

Let me tell you about another couple I know. The husband is the outdoorsy type. He works in an office, which just about kills him, where he makes good money to support the family. Every chance he gets, though, he heads out in a canoe or a kayak. He takes the kids with him. His wife rarely goes.

Their three children are involved in church activities, and he volunteers for the active ones (the kids' club sports, for instance). He's at church every Sunday in a suit, looking sharp. He greets people. He hosts Super Bowl parties. His wife, though, often looks miserable. She has confided in friends that he never prays or spiritually leads the family. She feels as if the spiritual responsibility for the family is all on her shoulders, and she resents it. She wants to submit—but she feels there's nothing to submit to!

I wonder if her idea of a spiritual leader and his idea of a spiritual leader are two different things. He is an involved dad. He makes sure his kids are at church. But his way of experiencing God is in the outdoors; it isn't in sitting around the table at night, reading a passage of Scripture, and discussing it.

When we say "spiritual leader," we often picture a father who calls the family together for a time that we are going to deem "our family devotions." But many men prefer to live out their faith in the things they do daily. It isn't necessarily wrong. It's just different.

My friend Derek isn't a "let's all sit around the table and read our Bibles" kind of dad either. But he is a spiritual person. He thinks deeply about current events, prays for his kids during his long commutes, and talks to his coworkers about God. His most spiritual moments with his boys, though, don't usually involve a Bible. They often involve a rifle. And orange coveralls. And a deer blind. And while he's huddling there, waiting with one of his sons for hours on end, they'll talk quietly about life and love, and he'll share his wisdom. And his boys learn what being a man of God is all about.

What If He Isn't a Spiritual Leader—in Any Way?

What if your husband doesn't go to church at all, though? What if he's not a spiritual leader in any sense?

If your husband doesn't want to go to church, that doesn't mean you shouldn't go. If your husband isn't interested in joining a Bible study and growing more in his faith (at least that's how you see it), that doesn't mean that you shouldn't.

I'm not sure why we believe that the husband must be the

stronger believer. "Spiritual leader" simply means that he sets the tone for the family and that ultimately he is responsible before God for his family's spiritual condition. It does not mean that if you have memorized more Scripture than he has, or that you know the Bible better than he does, then your family is out of God's design.

To hold yourself back because your husband isn't moving forward in his spiritual walk is an improper view of the Christian life and an improper view of Christian roles in marriage. We are each responsible individually before God. And if you get closer to God, you'll simply learn how to love your husband better anyway!

And what about leading the children spiritually? Blogger Jen Wilkin compares the spiritual leader role to her daily routine of walking her kids to school. Every day she walks them to the corner where a crossing guard, donning an orange vest and carrying a large stop sign, leads them safely across the street. Jen asks:

> Let's say for a minute that the crossing guard doesn't do
> her job one morning. Let's say she sees me coming with
> my little ones but decides to stay in her lawn chair scrolling
> through Instagram. Let's say that I ask her to help them
> across the intersection, but she ignores my valid request.
> What should I do? I don't have an orange vest or a stop
> sign. I don't know the traffic patterns like she does. Should
> I turn to my children and say, "Well, good luck—I'll pray
> you make it safely to the other side!"

Of course not. I should do what she has chosen not to
do. I should watch for an opening in the traffic and walk
my children safely across the street. I should submit to a
higher authority than the crossing guard in the interest of
doing what is safe and right.[9]

In everything, our ultimate submission is to God—we submit "as you are to the Lord" (Ephesians 5:22, NRSV). When we
lead our kids to God, we're doing so out of obedience to God.
When we pursue our husband's best, we're doing that to honor
God. When we refuse to follow our husbands into sin, we're honoring God. And when we joyfully follow where God is leading
our husbands, we do that to follow God too.

Let me leave you with Paul's words on how to build a happy,
unified marriage. In Colossians 3:12–15, Paul wrote:

> As God's chosen people, holy and dearly loved, clothe
> yourselves with compassion, kindness, humility, gentleness
> and patience. Bear with each other and forgive one another
> if any of you has a grievance against someone. Forgive as
> the Lord forgave you. And over all these virtues put on
> love, which binds them all together in perfect unity. Let
> the peace of Christ rule in your hearts, since as members
> of one body you were called to peace. And be thankful.

I can't think of a better prescription for achieving oneness
than that.

Summary of Action Steps

1. Pray about where God is leading your husband. Ask God, "How can I tangibly support my husband in that?"

2. Do a strength assessment in your marriage. Assign the jobs based on skills and preferences, not simply gender.

3. If you feel as if you may be enabling bad behavior, prayerfully read one of the boundary books listed in the appendix and apply what you learn.

4. Find a practical way every day to put your husband's needs and preferences first.

Thought #6

I'm Called to Be a Peacemaker, Not a Peacekeeper

Last year Leslie and Jim had to take out a second mortgage on their house to cover the credit card bills, and Leslie was panicking because they had just received notice that the electricity would be cut off in three weeks if the bill wasn't paid. Leslie wasn't sure how much they owed in total or if they had any money in the bank to prevent the lights from being switched off.

"I've tried to talk to Jim about it, and I've offered to take over the finances, but he gets upset and storms out. So I'm learning how to be quiet and be gentle and trust God that he will bring a solution," Leslie explained. Leslie understood money and debt better, but to Jim, giving up the finances was like saying he wasn't a man. So nothing ever got better.

"At least we're not fighting about it," Leslie said. "He just shuts down when we fight. So I've decided to let go and give this to God." Leslie was keeping the peace.

Pat Answer: *Fighting is poison to a marriage. Aim to live in peace instead. Avoid conflict at all costs.*

That may sound wise, but let's dissect it. What does it mean to live in peace? According to the 1979 Camp David Accords, Egypt and Israel are technically at peace. Many Egyptians, though, want that peace treaty shredded. Are they shooting at each other? No. But is there peace?

Thought #6: I'm called to be a peace*maker*, not a peace*keeper*.

In contrast, let's look at Canada (where I live) and the United States. We share a common culture and agree on basic things. We have trade agreements. We have military agreements. Northern states have even imported our Tim Hortons, which has far better coffee than Dunkin' Donuts. We're friends!

That's peace.

PURSUING PEACE DOESN'T MEAN PURSUING A LACK OF CONFLICT

Psalm 34:14 says, "Seek peace and pursue it." Seeking peace does not mean seeking an absence of conflict, like the Israelis and the Egyptians—or even, I believe, like Jim and Leslie. It means seeking a relationship characterized by mutual goodwill and understanding.

When Jesus was preparing to go to the cross, he prayed for his disciples (and for those of us who would come afterward). One of his prayers, from John 17, went like this: "My prayer is not for them alone. I pray also for those who will believe in me through their message, that all of them may be one, Father, just as you are in me and I am in you" (verses 20–21).

God's heart is always for oneness.

That sounds a little nebulous, though, doesn't it? How can we actually be "one"? Maybe if we read 1 Corinthians 1:10, we'll get a clearer picture. The apostle Paul wrote, "I appeal to you, dear brothers and sisters, by the authority of our Lord Jesus Christ, to live in harmony with each other. Let there be no divisions in the church. Rather, be of one mind, *united in thought and purpose*" (NLT).

That's why pursuing an absence of conflict strategy just doesn't cut it. You're not really agreeing with each other; you're just agreeing not to disagree. For decades leading up to the American Civil War, politicians were trying to avoid conflict. They came to all kinds of compromises regarding which states could have slaves and what they would do with fugitive slaves or with new territories. And none of it worked because the states were not united in truth. How can you forge real peace when you disagree on things that are so fundamental?

So what is it that God asks us to do? It's simple. Jesus said, "Blessed are the peacemakers, for they will be called children of God" (Matthew 5:9). Those who actually make peace are close to God's heart—so close that he calls them family. Making peace means pushing through a conflict until you get to the other side, where you can feel united in God. You understand each other. You feel intimate. You feel like one.

Avoiding conflict doesn't even compare.

When the apostles Paul and Peter were not united in thought and purpose, they called each other on it, they debated it, and in the end they made peace with each other. The scene was Antioch, where Paul spent much time after his initial conversion. Paul had been a Pharisee of the Pharisees: as strictly a by-the-book Law Guy as you can imagine. But when he met Christ, one of the first things that struck him was the huge implication of the gospel for reconciliation. It meant breaking down dividing walls, and that meant the Gentiles and Jews were now one.

Peter agreed with that. After all, he had received the vision of the sheet bearing all the unclean animals and God telling him to eat them—even though Jews would never have eaten those animals.[1] And then Peter had shared the gospel with Cornelius, a Gentile.

Yet when Peter visited Paul in Antioch, he stopped eating with Gentiles and only ate with Jews. And as Paul wrote in Galatians 2:11–14, Paul called Peter out on his hypocrisy. Paul's rebuke obviously made an impact, because when the Council in Jerusalem debated this issue a few years later, it was Peter who introduced Paul and Barnabas and who urged the Jewish Christians to listen to them (Acts 15:1–21). Paul and Peter had made peace. They were of one mind, on the same side.

But that peace was only possible because they talked through the issues. Had one of them said, "You have the authority here, and so I am not going to say anything even though I disagree," they would never have achieved this unity.

Sometimes the route to peace goes through conflict. No two

people will agree on everything, and when two different person-
alities, with different backgrounds and different expectations—
let alone different genders!—join together in marriage, they
will experience friction. But as we work through these things
and try to forge that oneness, we'll start to understand each other
better. We'll step outside of ourselves a bit. We'll grow more
loving.

It all sounds exactly like what Jesus wants us to do: to become
more like him.

Conflict Is Good for a Marriage

That's why conflict can actually be good for a marriage. I once
knew a gifted but very opinionated pastor who proudly told me
that he and his wife of forty years had never had a fight. I looked
at this sweet, quiet woman and wondered whether or not this was
a good thing. Perhaps all he meant was that they had never raised
their voices, but given his propensity to raise his voice from the
pulpit, that seemed unlikely. I think it far more likely that his wife
may have just swallowed her thoughts.

She was likely following the "Duck Principle." I've heard it
explained at women's retreats and on marriage and mom blogs,
and it goes something like this:

Pat Answer: *If you're upset at your spouse, state your
opinion, but then "duck" and get out of the way, so that
God can be the one to smack your husband, not you.*

I can remember one conference where we were handed little paper ducks to put in our Bibles, to remind us that it was not our job to point out any error in our husbands; it was only God's job. We were to "pray and get out of the way."

Leslie had really mastered that Duck thing. She was just like a little mallard, looking peaceful on the outside, while under the surface her legs were paddling frantically as she waited to see what would happen. After all, she'd ducked. So now God should smack her husband!

But let's look at it another way. If God's truth is timeless— and I believe it is—then we would expect that the things God wants also lead to better and healthier relationships. So if the healthiest thing were simply to "duck" and not express disagreement, then research should show that the best marriages are those in which there's little or no fighting. Actually, research shows the opposite. When Ernest Harburg of the University of Michigan looked into what makes a healthy marriage, he and his colleagues discovered that couples who express their anger live longer than couples who suppress it.[2]

The healthiest couples are not those where the wife states her position once and then ducks—or worse, never states her position in the first place. No, the happiest couples are those who wrestle through issues and don't back down until they rebuild intimacy and trust and closeness. In fact, conflict resolution contributes to healthier individuals in general, since people who suppress conflict actually die earlier. So peacemaking isn't just good for your marriage; it's good for your heart too!

Now there are healthy and unhealthy ways of fighting, and

I'm certainly not arguing that fighting for the sake of fighting or calling each other names or manipulating is a plus in marriage. And indeed, that's what Harburg found. Dealing with your anger well? Huge benefits. Yelling and throwing a fit? Not so much.

CONFLICT AND FIGHTING ARE NOT THE SAME

When many of us hear the word "conflict," we automatically imagine loud fighting.

Leslie grew up in an abusive household where people often got drunk, yelled, and threw things. She learned to become the "perfect child," to never stick her neck out, so that she wouldn't inadvertently trigger a fight. To Leslie, anger and disagreement are scary things. So she does all she can to make sure her husband doesn't feel angry.

Few of us grew up witnessing healthy conflict resolution, so it's no wonder many of us associate conflict with yelling and fighting and threatening the relationship. But conflict simply means two people coming together with opposing views. Conflict doesn't need to involve yelling (and indeed it shouldn't). Sometimes conflict may get heated; none of us is perfect, and when we're upset we may say things in a way that isn't particularly helpful. But while calling names and yelling is bad, airing a disagreement is actually good for your marriage.

Action Step: Think back to your childhood. What conflict resolution did you witness? Was anger a scary emotion that you wanted to avoid, or were conflicts handled well? If you can, think of a specific conflict when you were a child, and journal how your parents (or stepparents) reacted. Now compare this to how you react today.

Ruth Bell Graham, wife of the famous evangelist Billy, liked to say, "If two people agree on everything, one of them is unnecessary."[3] That clash of ideas and perspectives helps to refine us, and that's why conflict can actually be a blessing in your marriage. If you both always agree, then there is no "iron sharpening iron" (see Proverbs 27:17).

When my husband and I got married, my aunt and uncle gave us three top-of-the-line kitchen knives. I had never used quality knives before, and the first time I chopped carrots with them I laughed at how fast I could dice. But over the next two decades, either my reflexes grew slower or those knives started to wear out, because the carrots were refusing to dice as quickly. For my last birthday I told Keith I'd like some new knives.

One Saturday before our shopping spree, Keith was rummaging through our kitchen junk drawer when he came across this long, cylindrical metal object.

"What's this?" he asked.

I racked my brains trying to remember. "I think it may be a knife sharpener."

"Cool!" Keith said, and he immediately tried it out. Lo and behold, I could dice carrots again! Those knives simply needed to be sharpened, and the only way to do so was to rub them against more metal. Leave them on their own, with no friction, and knives become far less useful. We need to sharpen each other.

Unfortunately, many wives choose to swallow emotions, thinking that by doing so they are respecting their husbands and promoting peace. That isn't always the best route—in fact, I'd say that is *rarely* the best route. There are times we *should* just let things go (as we'll look at in Thought #7), but usually a dose of healthy conflict is better for everyone.

How can you feel "of one mind" with someone who does not know your heart? If you bottle things up, thinking that this makes you a better wife, you may be working directly against intimacy.

Action Step: Practice making your feelings known! If you tend to bottle up during conflict, afraid to express yourself, sometime this month, when you are in a group setting, express an opinion. Maybe it's at a small group, or at work, or at a committee meeting. Before everyone else chimes in, speak up!

PEACEMAKING: TWO MODELS OF CONFLICT RESOLUTION

Let's return to Leslie's story and see the two different models of dealing with conflict in action: the lack-of-conflict model and the peacemaking model.

Reacting with the Lack-of-Conflict Model

Leslie chose to respond to Jim by using the lack-of-conflict model. She "ducked." She told herself, *Jim is the leader in our relationship. I need to give him room to handle the finances without nagging him. I need to step back and put it in God's hands and not worry.*

So she said to Jim, "I'm sorry, honey. I didn't mean to put such pressure on you. I know you work hard for our family. I know you care about us. I respect you, I love you, and I know you will always provide and take care of us. I won't worry anymore." And she gave him a kiss and walked away. She took a deep breath and thanked God that he had her family in his hands and that he would always take care of them.

Did she make peace? She did, after all, give up the issue. She left the ball in Jim's court, and she didn't demand he do anything else. The electricity bill did get paid, but other bills were still outstanding. And she still had no idea of their actual financial situation. Likewise, Jim knew that his wife said she wouldn't bug him, but he also knew that he hadn't provided and the finances were a mess. Because of that he still felt defensive, she still felt anxious, and they were not at peace.

Reacting with the Peacemaking Model

In the peacemaking model, the goal is to understand each other and work through the challenge so that you grow more intimate. Unfortunately, this wasn't the route Leslie chose. But Lily did.

On her blog, *The Respect Dare,* author Nina Roesner shared the story of an unnamed woman I'll call "Lily," who was in the same situation as Leslie, but who realized that peacemaking was more important than peacekeeping.

Lily had been acting like Leslie: she tried to respect her husband and let him take leadership. But in Lily's case, the electricity actually did get cut off. Her husband wasn't handling their finances responsibly. Lily had believed that the best way to honor her husband was to willingly let him take the lead with their finances. Unfortunately, he wasn't leading. And the whole family was suffering for it.

When the electricity was turned off, Lily faced a crisis point. She finally realized she was standing in the way of allowing him to feel the consequences of his behavior. She said, "The truth was that his lack of wisdom, his lack of maturity, his foolishness, negatively impacted his kids and me. I had hid that from him in the name of being a 'good' wife. I protected him from it because I didn't want to hurt his feelings. And he took advantage of me, and I let him, and I realized I wasn't being good but rather NICE."[4]

A good wife is concerned about the same thing God is concerned about: her husband's character. If she covers for him because she wants to be nice, then she is disrupting the "law of sowing and reaping," just as Adeline did in her story in Thought #4.

A woman in Lily's situation may need to tell her husband: "I love you, but you cannot continue to place our family in financial jeopardy. I am happy to take over the finances if you would prefer. If you would like to continue to handle them, though, then I need to tell you that if bills don't get paid and our housing situation is in jeopardy, I will have to find a safer place for me and the children to live while this is sorted out."

Sometimes we focus so much on not causing any conflict or on submitting to our husbands—on being "nice"—that we actually work directly against building intimacy and being "good."

A peacekeeper simply avoids conflict. When there's a disagreement, she retreats. A peacemaker is aiming for much more: she wants reconciliation. And reconciliation is active, not passive.

Action Step: Decide with your husband what your "conflict rules" will be. Examples may be: don't leave the house during a disagreement; don't have a huge disagreement in front of the children; give ourselves half an hour to think and pray before we discuss; pray first.

In Thought #7 I'll give some practical guidelines on how to work through conflict in a healthy way. Not all disagreements, after all, are as serious as Leslie and Jim's, or Lily's. More often than not, our conflicts are more mundane, about hurt feelings, misunderstandings, and busy schedules. Some of us, though, are walking through really difficult conflicts where some major sin is involved. Your spouse is doing something that is endangering the marriage—and his own soul. Let's turn now to being a peacemaker in these difficult situations.

PEACEMAKING: RESOLVING CONFLICT WHEN DANGEROUS SINS ARE PRESENT

I heard the story recently of a woman whose husband had been addicted to porn for years. They had visited counselors, and he had promised he would stop but he hadn't. Finally, she told a few select people in her small group and the elders at her church, and the elders confronted her husband and told him they were supporting a separation. The members of the small group helped the wife pack her things and find an apartment. The couple has not divorced; they are separated. But she has tried everything else and it hasn't worked, and now her church is backing her as she puts her husband in a situation where he has to choose: *Will I do the right thing and follow God? Or will I turn away?*

Just after I heard this story, I received this e-mail:

> I discovered my husband's porn stash a few months after we were married. I confronted him about it, and he told me that he quit porn, but he never did. Every few months I would catch him watching something, or I would find stuff on his computer.
>
> We rarely had sex because he preferred the porn to me. I would cry and yell, and he would say he would get better but he never has. He's a smart guy and he's had good jobs, but he was fired from one ten years ago for using his work computer for porn. And then two months ago he was fired from a great job because he racked up porn charges on his company phone.
>
> I'm learning how to be gracious and patient and how to love my husband, even when he seems unlovable. What makes me so sad, though, is that we've basically had no sex life, and because of that we have no kids. And now I'm in my late thirties and I'm afraid it's too late. But I'm still just praying, "God, one day at a time. Show me that I'm lovable." And God always does.

Two stories of porn use going on for decades. Which woman used the peacemaking model: the one who decided to confront the sin and separate, or the one who focused on learning patience daily as she did little about her husband's sin? Sometimes we think we're doing the spiritual thing by ducking and "giving it to God," but what if God wants us to use the tools and the steps that he's already laid out for us? Submission means putting the other person's well-being first, and that includes their spiritual well-being. If we sit back and wait for God to convict our husbands, are we seeking peace? Or are we using theological arguments to avoid doing the hard work of peacemaking?

> **Pat Answer:** *A woman's role is to "win him without words." Your job is not to correct him; it's to be a shining example of righteousness that will point him toward God.*

Some commenters on my blog suggest that the Bible tells women who are being verbally abused to "win him without words." (I tend to delete those comments!) Others have suggested that whatever a husband's sin, God's strategy for wives is to be shining, silent examples. They point to 1 Peter 3:1–2, where Peter instructed women to "submit yourselves to your own husbands so that, if any of them do not believe the word, they may be won over without words by the behavior of their wives, when they see the purity and reverence of your lives." These verses, though, have nothing to do with conflict. The "won over without words" is about winning an unbeliever to Christ, not about a strategy to stop someone from making bad decisions or being abusive. Yet too often I find that women who are already uncomfortable with conflict take these verses as an excuse to avoid necessary conversations. Covering for sin does not help someone grow spiritually; it allows that sin to grow instead. That's why this pat answer often backfires too:

Pat Answer: *Give your problems to God. Leave them at the foot of the cross, and God will take care of them.*

"Leaving them at the foot of the cross" feels as though you're exercising trust, but sometimes stepping out in faith shows more trust than standing back and doing nothing. And stepping out in faith is intrinsic to peacemaking. To figure out why this may be, we've got to unpack the idea of "peacemaking" down to one more level. Earlier I said that it was creating a relationship where you felt of one mind, united in thought and purpose under Jesus. We've talked about being united in thought and purpose; now I want to look at what it means to be united under Jesus.

MAKING JESUS THE BASIS OF OUR UNITY

Being united in thought and purpose is actually meaningless if we're united to the *wrong* thought and purpose. Islamic terror groups are perfectly united in thought and purpose to attack those who do not agree with their virulent strain of Islam, but we wouldn't say that they are peacemakers. The staff at abortion clinics may be completely united in thought and purpose, but we wouldn't call them peacemakers either. *What* you're united under matters.

So what do you do if your husband is doing something that is seriously jeopardizing his peace with God—and with his family? Well, God tells us how to deal with it in Matthew 18:15–17:

> If your brother or sister sins, go and point out their fault, just between the two of you. If they listen to you, you have won them over. But if they will not listen, take one or two others along, so that "every matter may be established by the testimony of two or three witnesses." If they still refuse to listen, tell it to the church; and if they refuse to listen even to the church, treat them as you would a pagan or a tax collector.

You talk to him first, and if that doesn't work, you go and get two others to talk to him, and if that still doesn't work, you talk to the church. Of the two women whose husbands were involved in porn, only one took this route.

Sometimes we cannot make peace alone, and God knows this. Jesus even gave us a blueprint of what to do when we can't agree together. We're supposed to lean on other people.

In the first few verses of Philippians 4, this theme of "oneness" and resolving conflict pops up again. Paul wrote in verse 2, "I plead with Euodia and I plead with Syntyche to be of the same mind in the Lord." There's that oneness—being united in thought and purpose—that we talked about. But then Paul went on and said in verse 3, "Yes, and I ask you, my true companion, *help these women* since they have contended at my side in the cause of the gospel." Sometimes we need other people to help us make peace and achieve oneness.

Do you think the Bible meant for this to be true for every relationship *except* marriage? Was God saying, "Work through your conflict with people. Confront issues. Unless, of course, you're a woman, and then you should only do so with absolutely everyone *except* your husband"? Of course not! God was giving us principles on how to deal with disagreements, and sometimes that involves bringing in a third party.

WHEN SHOULD I INVOLVE SOMEONE ELSE?

We all sin. Maybe we gossip too much or we're prideful or we watch some inappropriate movies. I'm certainly not saying that you should run to other people every time you see your husband commit a sin. Imagine if he did that to you! But sometimes a sin is so big that it can't be ignored.

I'm afraid that in the church we feel as if we can't properly confront these sins because to do so sometimes seems as if we may jeopardize the marriage itself. And God hates divorce, after all!

Yes, he does. But do you know what he hates more? People jeopardizing their souls.

Churches should be places where the wounded find healing, not where the wounded find cover so they can avoid healing. And yet too often that is what we've done. We hate divorce so much that we ignore the other side: God does not want an army of wounded, damaged people; he wants wholeness. When a spouse is endangering his or her relationship with the family and with God, something must be done. And if nothing is done, then the spouse is giving cover to the sin.

I know it's scary to ask for help. It requires humility to tell someone else that your marriage is messed up. It's even harder if you're in ministry or your husband is in ministry. But let's not forget the bigger picture: What does it help to gain the whole world, but lose your soul (Matthew 16:26)? So let me outline five things I commonly see in marriages that warrant outside intervention.

Affairs

If your husband is having an affair, you need to get help. If he has been flirting with other women on Facebook or pursuing an emotional relationship with someone else, you may also need outside help to talk through issues and provide for him accountability. And because affairs are so painful to recover from, you'll need someone, perhaps a counselor, to walk through the healing process with you too.

Abuse

If your husband is physically abusing you, please get out and call the police at once. Abuse should never be tolerated. Submission doesn't mean that you allow someone to mistreat you. Real submission points people to God; it does not enable sin. But what if the abuse isn't physical—what if it's verbal or emotional? And how can you tell the difference between verbal abuse and just a normal fight in marriage?

If you feel as if you have to walk on eggshells constantly to prevent your husband from blowing up, there is likely a deep problem in your marriage. If he regularly calls you names, belittles you, or criticizes you, there is something seriously wrong. Unfortunately, many pastors don't know how to handle this type of abuse, but counselors can often identify it. If you fear you may be in an abusive situation, please seek out a counselor. Also, please check out the appendix to this book where I list other resources to help you identify these types of relationships.

Addictions

Addictions of all types—financial, emotional, physical—can wreak havoc with your husband's ability to be completely present for the family. We're used to hearing about the dangers posed by chemical dependencies, like drug and alcohol problems. Yet porn, video game, and gambling compulsions can also be harmful. If you feel that your husband is no longer able to function well in his daily life because of his dependence on something mood-altering, seeking help is the best course of action.

Sexual Refusal

Is sex almost nonexistent in your marriage? Usually when it's the man who withdraws from sex, porn is involved. Sometimes, though, sexual withdrawal is caused by major psychological and emotional damage. Maybe there are homosexual tendencies, or maybe your husband has pushed down his sexuality so that he becomes passive and asexual. He could also be embarrassed or disheartened by sexual issues, like erectile dysfunction or low testosterone.

If a spouse rejects sex, he is specifically rejecting community, as well as rejecting a huge part of himself. Paul said in 1 Corinthians 7:4–5:

The wife's body does not belong to her alone but also to her husband. In the same way, the husband's body does not belong to him alone but also to his wife. Do not deprive each other except by mutual consent and for a time, so that you may devote yourselves to prayer. Then come together again so that Satan will not tempt you because of your lack of self-control. (NIV, 1984)

Sex is not an optional part of marriage, and yet too many of us are living in sexless marriages, thinking we can do nothing about it.

Sexual refusal can't be ignored, and a person who has become asexual must be confronted and told, "You need to get counseling or see a doctor." Nothing is wrong with having psychological trauma or physical issues; there *is* something wrong with refusing to deal with these things.

Financial Endangerment

I received an e-mail from a wife recently who said this:

For the last four years my husband has refused to work. When he did work he often called in sick, and was always searching out ways to apply for disability. Now he just sits at home and plays video games all day. We lost our house, and I'm working two part-time jobs to try to pay the bills, plus keeping the house clean and doing his laundry. He won't work! What do I do?

A man who refuses to provide for his family and who has become this lazy also needs Christians to come alongside him and encourage him firmly to act responsibly. The same would be true for a spouse who is consistently getting the family deep into debt with spending. Sometimes a man may not actually be lazy; he may be struggling with debilitating depression or psychological trauma, which saps his drive to do much of anything. Even if laziness isn't the issue, the underlying cause still needs to be addressed for the family's health and for the husband's health.

If your spouse is acting in such a way that he is denying a vital part of himself and a vital part of the Christian life—such as responsibility or intimacy or community—then doing nothing about it enables that spouse to avoid any impetus for spiritual growth.

WHO DO I ASK FOR HELP?

The passage in Matthew 18 does not say, "Tell all your friends and ask their advice," or "Go running to your parents." It does say to tell two or three believers—and only two or three—initially. I'd suggest talking to a couple you respect, who you know can keep things confidential, and who can come to your house and listen to both sides of the story and hold you both accountable. A couple is ideal because you've got another male who can exert influence on your husband and a woman who can help you find a healthy perspective. If that isn't feasible or you have no one to ask, then I'd talk to a pastor or a counselor.

Action Step: Identify a couple whom you can go to for advice, and ask if they will mentor you. Before a conflict even starts, find a couple who can talk with you and pray with you, so that when they're needed, you already have a relationship with them.

In *Rocking the Roles,* Robert Lewis told the story of an intervention at his church. A woman was married to a financially reckless man. She was working hard to keep the family afloat, but she couldn't manage it anymore because of his spending.[5]

The elders came alongside the man and said (and I'm paraphrasing), "We are going to help you make a budget. Then you are going to stick to it. You'll report to one of us every week until this is all sorted out. And if you continue to overspend, we all will show up at the house with a moving van and we will help your wife and your kids get established in a house of their own until you come to your senses."

They weren't advocating a divorce; they were saying, "What you are doing is so unacceptable that you must stop. And if you won't, you alone will bear the consequences because we will help your wife through this."

Now, elders should never do anything this drastic until they hear both sides of the story. But once that story is clear, if one spouse is consistently damaging the family and damaging his or her own spiritual life, then action simply must be taken to make peace under God.

Find someone who will walk you through an intervention process, if it is necessary, and someone who will stand alongside your husband and give him the tools and help he needs to rediscover who he was made to be. I know this is scary. You're shifting the balance, and it feels as if you're the one disturbing the peace. But this is how we make peace, and it's so much better than ducking and letting huge issues fester.

Summary of Action Steps

1. Think of a conflict from your childhood, and journal about how your parents/stepparents handled it. Does this give you insights into how you handle conflict?

2. Speak up! In a group setting this month, chime in with your opinion before others share theirs.

3. Identify rules with your husband for how you will handle conflict.

4. Ask a couple to serve as your mentors.

Thought #7

Being One Is More Important Than Being Right

I brought major rejection baggage into my marriage. Add my fiery personality that loved to debate, and suddenly normal marital conflict ballooned into an epic battle of the wills. I was determined to win every fight. I listened intently whenever we had a conflict, just as you're supposed to. But instead of listening to understand, I was listening for the loopholes.

If Keith said something like, "You never just tell me what you like about me. You're always criticizing me," I would rejoice. Those words gave me my opening, because he had said "never" and "always." All I had to do was find an exception and I could leave his argument in the dust!

I figured that if I could show Keith that all the reasons he had for feeling hurt and angry were totally stupid, then he would stop being hurt and angry. He would realize how good he had it, and he would never want to leave me. In retrospect I know that sounds absurd, but somewhere in the back of my mind it made sense to me.

Conflict handled well can be helpful to a marriage, but our conflict drove us further and further apart, because Keith would feel more and more distant and more and more unloved. We never actually resolved anything since we weren't really dealing with the issues. I focused on winning the argument, but in the process I was losing my husband. I forgot that marriage was not about me winning; marriage was about oneness—and that meant we needed to find a way for both of us to win.

Thought #7:
Being one is more important than being right.

WHAT'S THE GOAL?

As we discussed in Thoughts #5 and #6, the goal of conflict is to emerge feeling that you're of one mind and one purpose, that you're on the same page. When you're angry, though, the first thing to pop into your head usually is not *How can we find common ground?* Instead, it's *How can I make him see how much he's hurting me?*

Anger does that to us. We don't want to get on the same page; we want him to get on *our* page. And so we go into attack mode. But that's not going to build oneness.

The problem is not with anger. It's with whether we allow that anger to distract us from the goal of building intimacy. Jesus himself got angry on numerous occasions, but he never let that anger detract from his goal of spreading the good news of the kingdom of God. He used his anger in constructive ways.

One of the problems in Jesus's day was that unscrupulous businessmen would try to make money off religious pilgrims arriving at the temple in Jerusalem offer sacrifices. They would charge huge prices to change currencies to buy the ritual sacrifices, making it harder for the poor to do what God required. When Jesus saw this firsthand, he got mad.

The story is told in all four Gospels, but Mark's account is especially interesting because of this little tidbit: One Sunday, Jesus entered Jerusalem on a donkey (fulfilling the messianic prophecy about him told in Zechariah 9:9), and the crowds all yelled, "Hosanna in the highest!" (Mark 11:10). Then verse 11 recounts that "Jesus entered Jerusalem and went into the temple courts. He looked around at everything, but since it was already late, he went out to Bethany with the Twelve."

The next morning Jesus walked back to Jerusalem, heading for the temple. "He overturned the tables of the money changers and the benches of those selling doves" (verse 15). Why is this important for us to know?

Because before he did anything, he slept on it. He thought about it. He prayed about it. John even recounted that he made a whip out of cords (John 2:15). I can picture Jesus sitting around the fire the night before, talking to his disciples, and weaving the cord as he's thinking about what he would do the next day. This wasn't an impulsive act; the next morning he was ready to confront those abusing the temple and put things right, so that people could worship freely again. It was all about restoring right relationship with God for the people. He used his anger to help solve a problem.

Restoring My Relationship Must Be the Goal

Remembering your goal is tough, though, because when you're mad, adrenaline starts surging. Thinking clearly when you're angry is almost impossible because of all the chemical reactions going on inside your brain. When you feel threatened, your brain enters a "fight or flight" response, where blood flow rushes to the brain and out of your extremities. Your heart rate increases. Your body gets primed to flee, if needed. All of your senses are heightened. This cycle starts because the limbic system takes over, inhibiting rational thinking and putting you into emergency mode. It often takes up to an hour after feeling anger for the cerebral cortex, the part of the brain responsible for higher order thinking, to start functioning normally again.

Empathy can speed up that normalization process. When we choose to step outside of ourselves and recognize that the other person in front of us is our ally, we can halt that chemical reaction and stop the "fight or flight" response. That's because deliberately making the choice to feel empathy activates the cerebral cortex. When we access that, we can slow the "fight or flight" response and bring back rational thinking.

It's like the climactic battle scene in *The Lord of the Rings: The Two Towers*. Aragorn and dwarf Gimli are swinging their sword and ax respectively at everything that moves, cutting down the enemy. All of a sudden they find themselves facing each other, and they draw up their weapons, ready to strike, when they recognize the person in front of them. They stop in their tracks. They see not foe, but friend. The battle frenzy dissipates.

When you're in the middle of a conflict and the anger starts going, you have a choice. You can see the person in front of you as an ally, or you can continue fighting, lashing out, and trying to win.

The most effective way of seeing your husband as an ally is to stop and pray and ask God to help both of you see clearly. My husband does this regularly—and in the heat of anger it often annoys me. I want to make my point, and somehow I know that if we bring God in, I won't be able to fight as effectively. God may not share my viewpoint, after all! But when Keith prays, that feeling that "I need to win" is halted almost immediately. Prayer is humbling; it reminds us that there is a God deserving of our worship, whose will is far more important than our own. It's hard to stay in that "fight or flight" anger when we see ourselves standing with our husband, both under God. I'm glad I have a husband who is able to be rational, even when I'm tempted to let emotions take over.

Action Step: When anger flares, pray separately, or together if possible, "God, help me to have your mind about this situation. Help us to find the solution that honors you and respects each other. Help me to see what I must do to fix this rift."

YOUR SPOUSE IS NOT THE PROBLEM

Realizing you're allies is a good first step, but for conflict to be effective in building oneness you must actually resolve the issue.

That's a thornier challenge because the issue you're fighting about is not always obvious. In the heat of the moment when you're feeling angry or hurt, if I were to ask you what the issue was, you'd probably answer, "He isn't listening to me!" "He's making unreasonable demands!" "He's not paying attention to the kids!" You'd begin every sentence with "He."

That's the crux of the problem. When the issue is always with the other person, then you're still in win-lose mode. When the problem is "him," then the only way to end the conflict is to defeat "him."

Let's use a practical example to show what happens when both spouses assume the other is wrong.

Recently I received this e-mail from a reader:

I'm seven months pregnant and I have two-year-old twins. And I'm exhausted. My husband and I have been renting a small apartment for the last few years, and we need to get out by the beginning of next month. There's a small house we could buy now and then be settled once and for all, but my husband would rather move into another rental and keep looking for properties for the next few months. I can handle moving once, but I don't think I can handle moving twice. What do I do? He doesn't seem to have any concept of how tired I am.

Her husband is prioritizing the long term: *We want to build a house, so let's just sacrifice for the next few months and get what we really want at the right time. What's a few months?* The wife, on the other hand, is focusing on the short term: *I have a baby coming, I'm tired, and I need to be settled.*

Both are valid perspectives.

Often during conflict, though, the couple attacks each other's *interpretation* of the situation rather than identifying the feelings that are making this situation problematic in the first place. In this scenario, the couple starts debating the pros and cons of buying a house right now.

Imagine how that conversation will go: She'll insist that she's just too tired to move twice and that they really need to settle down. He'll tell her that will be more work in the long run, because it will end up costing them money and they won't be as happy. And they'll go around and around and get more and more frustrated, because the real issue is not real estate. As it is with most conflicts, the real issue is that they both have different unmet physical or emotional needs. Identify those needs, and you can find the win-win.

Our e-mail writer's need is to feel protected and not overwhelmed. Her husband, on the other hand, needs to feel financially secure. What would happen if they started talking about *those* issues instead?

If you phrase the problem in terms of needs you both have, then instead of being in "anger" mode and blaming each other, you can enter "problem solving" mode, where you brainstorm all the different ways you can meet those needs. It's no longer a question of who will win the argument. It's a question of how can you do things differently so both you and your spouse feel valued, safe, and loved.

Early in our homeschooling life when our girls were in first and third grades, my husband and I faced a crisis. He was a busy pediatrician, on call two or three nights a week and in the office every weekday. Time as a family was scarce. I was busy with the girls, but my writing career was also blossoming. I had just received a book contract and needed time to write.

Meanwhile, Keith was approaching burnout. He desperately needed some time to relax. And one of his favorite hobbies is re-enacting historical battles using miniature soldiers. Sounds super geeky, I know, but our small town boasts a bunch of guys who love doing this too, and Keith wanted one night a week to join them.

I experienced that request as a personal affront, and the anger started to build. The house and the kids were all my responsibility. I had put my career on hold so that he could go to medical school and open his practice, but I needed an intellectual outlet too. I wanted time to pursue my own career, and he was trying to take time for a hobby on top of the career he already had.

Didn't he respect my career goals? Didn't he realize that I needed some time away from the kids too? But he was equally desperate: Didn't I realize that he needed some downtime, especially since he dealt with life-and-death issues that were wearing on him?

We went around in circles until Keith stopped us.

"Sheila, we're being ridiculous," he said. "I know you love me and want me to have free time, and you know I love you and want to see your writing grow. We just have a *time* problem, that's all."

When he put it like that, we were no longer in attack mode. We were in problem-solving mode. And that was so much better!

Many marriages get stuck in these conflicts because spouses approach conflict in "win-lose" mode. You both want opposite things, so obviously only one can "win." Either Keith had time to play with the guys, or I had time to write. Instead, prepare the groundwork so that it's easier to find the "win-win." Identify the real issues (feelings and needs), and then make a game plan for how you will problem solve and find that win-win.

Action Step: Identify your unmet needs.

Ask yourself, "What do I need in this situation right now?" When you find the answer, you've named your issue—your unmet need—and that means you can start problem solving. You're not debating whether or not the other person has a right to feel angry or whether the other person is right or wrong. You're focusing on your needs.

Action Step: Write your unmet needs on a piece of paper, and encourage your spouse to do the same. Now sit beside each other, with the papers in front of you, and decide whose "needs" to tackle first.

You could certainly just state your need out loud, but I like the idea of writing it down. It clarifies what you're talking about, so you don't go off on tangents and bring up everything under the sun that your husband has ever done to disappoint you. You only address the issues on the papers.

Also, by writing it on a piece of paper, the issue is now separate from you. Place those pieces of paper on the table in front of you so that you are sitting beside your husband, as a team. You're tackling them together; you're not tackling each other. As Zig Ziglar once said, "Many marriages would be better if the husband and wife clearly understood that they're on the same side."[1] I think that's brilliant.

PROBLEM SOLVE TO FIND THE WIN-WIN

After Keith identified our time problem, we stopped fighting over who should get time off, and we took a step back. Keith legitimately needed time with his friends. I legitimately needed an extra half-day a week to myself to write. So we asked ourselves: How can we find that time? We threw out different ideas, from getting baby-sitters to putting the girls in school, until we found a different solution. We decided that we valued time more than money. Keith decided to close his office on Thursday afternoons so he could homeschool the girls, something he wanted to do anyway, and then I could write. And every Tuesday night, a pile of guys rang our doorbell and headed downstairs to act out the Civil War.

If my letter writer and her husband could brainstorm about their needs, they could likely come up with some creative ways to figure out their housing situation too. She's worried about feeling overwhelmed and having to move twice. Certainly they could just move once, as she wanted. But perhaps other options exist. If it will save them money in the long run to rent just one more time, could they spend some of that money to hire a housekeeper? Could they ask one of their moms to visit? Could they hire a niece or a younger sibling to come and live in the house after the baby arrives to care for the twins? Could they hire a moving company to pack up all of their stuff instead of relying on her to do it?

And what about his need for financial security? There are different ways to meet this need too. They could rent and then decide to build this year, as he wants. But perhaps they could also look at whether they could move to a cheaper community. They could look at their expenses for opportunities to cut back. They could try finding him a better job.

When you're facing a conflict, ask yourselves: What are the different ways that we can meet each other's needs? Think of as many possibilities as you can, and then decide which ones you'll pursue. Write down all your ideas if you're list-type people, or go for a walk and talk if you'd prefer just to hash it out together. You can even exchange the pieces of paper, and take a day and think about those list items before agreeing to come back together to discuss everything.

Let's look at another common example to see how this problem-solving method of conflict resolution may play out. A woman wrote to me and described an area of disagreement:

I hate housework. My definition of clean is more like tidy. Even that, though, is a stretch for me.

Once my husband and I were married, I would pick up after both of us. Doing our laundry, cooking our dinners—everything that I figured would make him think I could be a good housewife. But that's not me. So when my husband would travel on business, I began living in my house the way I normally would. When my husband would come home on the weekends, I'd make a mad dash on Friday to clean the house because I knew he would freak out.

Now we're having it out because he is home and gets to see that my daily routine doesn't include cleaning. He's really upset by this and wants me to clean more, but I don't feel like that's me. And we can't seem to come to a compromise. I think it's my house too, and I need to be allowed to set some of the standards. What should we do to get past our conflict over housework?

What's the underlying issue this couple is facing? On the surface, it looks as if the problem is agreeing about how clean the house should be. Think about what would happen if they started to have that discussion, though. It would inevitably go downhill fast because they simply disagree. She thinks there's nothing wrong with clutter, and he thinks the house should be spick-and-span all the time. There's no way to win that conflict.

Most marital conflicts aren't about the issue you seem to be disagreeing about. They're about the fundamental questions: Do you really love me? Do you value my opinion? Do you care? In this case, the husband wants to know, "Do you care what I think about the house enough to leave your comfort zone?" And the wife also wants to know of the husband, "Do you care what I like enough to leave *your* comfort zone?" It's hardly surprising that they both dig in, because the root of the disagreement is not how clean the house is. The root is that they both don't feel valued.

If the couple starts conflict with prayer, inviting God in, they're immediately humbled. They stop demanding, "Will you change?" and start asking, "What is my role in fixing this?" Now they can start addressing the issue by writing their needs down. In this case, several needs may be at play. Both spouses need to know: "Do you really love me?" And both of them also need to feel "at home" while at home.

Her piece of paper may look something like this:

- I need to feel like this is my home.
- I need to feel like you do care about me and respect me, not that you think I'm some sort of child because I don't clean the house well.

His may look like this:

- I need to be able to relax when I come home.
- I need to feel that my opinion matters to you.

It may still appear as if the couple has a major problem: they both want to feel "at home" when they're at home, and neither of them currently does. But by writing their needs down, it's clear that they *both* have the right to want to feel at home. And now they can problem solve together to find the win-win.

My friend Terri had a similar difference of opinion with her husband. Terri was a busy homeschooling mom of six who loved creating a fun, unstructured place to learn. She wanted the children to be creative with art, explore nature, and run experiments. The house was always chaotic.

That bothered her husband, Jonathan, who felt like a stranger in his own house. He didn't have a place to sit when he came home from work because the kids' stuff spilled out all over the furniture. After a busy day, he longed to enter the front door and feel peace. Instead he felt immediately agitated.

At first their conversation was unproductive. Terri wanted Jonathan to value learning as she did, and to recognize that with six kids home all day, of course it would get messy! Jonathan wanted Terri to recognize that as the dad, he should also have a say in the "feel" of the house.

Finally they came up with a unique solution that I now recommend to couples: Pick your top five must-haves. If you and your spouse are diametrically opposed on something like how clean the house should be, ask yourself, *What are the top five things that would make me feel that my needs are being considered?* In Jonathan's case, he wanted the entryway clean when he walked in the door. He wanted a couch completely cleared off so he could sit down and put his feet up. He wanted the bed made. He wanted the dinner dishes washed every night. And he wanted the table set. Terri decided she could easily do those things. And then when Jonathan came in the door, he did feel peace, even if microscopes and butterfly carcasses still littered the coffee table.

My letter writer and her husband could each write down their own "Five Must-Haves" as well. He may have five areas of the home, as Jonathan did, that he wants to have tidy. She, on the other hand, may have her own five things that help her feel at home. She may want to leave her knitting in the living room; go a day or two without folding all the laundry or putting it away; cover the refrigerator with magnets and pictures; allow the kids to keep their play area messy; and keep her bottles and tubes on the bathroom counter. When you see the world in polar opposite ways, identifying your "Five Must-Haves" is a great strategy to honor both perspectives.

Action Step: Brainstorm all the ways that you can each meet the unmet needs, and decide which ones you will pursue.

PROBLEM SOLVING THE "LOVE" ISSUE

Early in a marriage, most conflict takes on far more significance than the issue would seem to warrant, because what's really being debated is, "Will you change for me? Will you care about me enough to accept me the way I am and accommodate me?" Whether the issue is housecleaning or sex or when to have kids or which careers to pursue, the underlying problem is often that we're unsure if we're really loved.

When you're problem solving, then, it's always a good idea to tackle that underlying issue as well: How can I help you to feel loved? Learning each other's love languages can aid in this. Gary Chapman has identified five love languages in which we tend to express love to others: quality time, words of affirmation, acts of service, physical touch, and gifts.[2] Each of us tends to experience love in one, or maybe two, primary ways.

The ways that we experience love tend also to be the ways that we like to express it. However, this can often backfire. Gifts, for instance, don't even register on my love language meter. I don't appreciate them. Acts of service, though, are heaven to me. If my husband keeps coming home with flowers but never does the dishes, I don't feel loved, even if he thinks that's what he's communicating. On the other hand, he's recently learned that a massage at night does wonders for my mood—and my libido! For him to take fifteen minutes and work at the knots on my back means so much to me, especially since I naturally carry so much tension in my upper torso. I've also learned that greeting him at the door, though such a simple thing, makes a huge difference in how loved he feels.

Figure out what says "love" to your husband, and then make it a habit to show love in these ways every day.

Action Step: Learn each other's love languages, and then translate that into tangible ideas. Each of you write a list of things that make you feel loved, and then exchange lists.

I know conflict resolution is not always as neat and tidy as I've presented it. Sometimes emotions do get the better of us. Sometimes we each have a hard time listening. That's okay. Just keep practicing, and you'll find that over time you'll become a pro. If it doesn't work the first time, don't despair. Keep praying and asking God to help you keep your cool and see your spouse as an ally. And then, when you're calmed down, pull out those pieces of paper and try again!

WHAT IF SOMEONE'S NEED IS ILLEGITIMATE?

The examples of conflict I've given have something in common: no case has a morally right answer; they all just have different perspectives. What if your conflict isn't so neat? What if, in your case, there is a moral issue at play?

Let's say, for instance, that your husband chats frequently with an ex-girlfriend on Facebook. Or perhaps your spouse is keeping secrets, and you can't get him to open up. Here's a comment that a pastor's wife left on my blog:

> Ten years ago I found out that my (pastor) husband of
> twenty-five years was addicted to pornography. He was
> repentant, and we worked on healing our marriage. After
> a year, we pretty much put it behind us and we never
> brought it up. A few months ago I asked him how he was
> doing with his porn problem. He became upset. I asked
> him a little later and told him that I really needed to know
> if he has looked at porn since. He said he is not having a
> problem, but refuses to get accountability or to give me
> the passwords to his computer or phone. I don't know if I
> should just trust him or if I should pursue it.

In this case, if the couple were to write out their needs, his might say something like this:

- I need to feel as if you trust me.
- I need to feel as if I have some privacy.

Trust and privacy sound like legitimate needs, but it depends on what we mean by them. To come back to Micah 6:8, we are to act justly, to love mercy, and to walk humbly with our God. Acting justly means that we stand up for justice, not that we ignore injustice. If a person wants privacy so they can cover a sin, that is not a legitimate need. Yes, privacy and trust are important, but once you're married, you also owe your spouse complete honesty and openness. Some things that we believe are needs, then, are not necessarily legitimate. No one needs a license to sin.

These are the sorts of needs that are legitimate (though this isn't a complete list):

- I need to feel that I am a priority to you.
- I need to feel that you love me.
- I need to spend time with you.
- I need to have some time to myself (the good kind of privacy!).
- I need to get enough rest and not be overworked.
- I need to feel financially secure (within reason).
- I need to feel as if I matter to you.
- I need to be able to share my thoughts and feelings with you.
- I need to know you respect me.
- I need to feel safe.
- I need help parenting, so that I'm not doing it all alone.
- I need to feel as if we are a team (the good kind of trust!).
- I need to know that my sexual needs matter to you.

- I need to know that I am the only object of sexual desire that you have.

The following things, though, are not always legitimate needs:

- I need privacy to do what I want without interference.
- I need to be able to do what I want with my own time.
- I need to feel as if you trust me automatically, no matter what.
- I need you to treat me like an adult and not question my choices.
- I need to be allowed to talk to whomever I want, whenever I want.
- I need to have a sexual outlet, and if you won't provide it, I need to be able to find it myself.

What happens when our lists collide? One of you may have a legitimate need: *I need to feel that I am your only object of sexual desire.* The other spouse may have another need that isn't legitimate: *I need privacy to do what I want without interference.*

Where does that leave you?

Our culture says something like this:

Cultural Message: *All feelings are legitimate and must be validated. In marriage, the spouse always has a right to his or her feelings.*

Interestingly, I've heard Christian counselors make the same argument. Feelings are an intrinsic part of a person's autonomy, and we must not pooh-pooh them or dismiss them if the relationship is to be healthy.

I understand the argument, and on its face it makes sense. But it doesn't quite jibe with Jeremiah 17:9: "The heart is deceitful above all things and beyond cure." If the heart is wicked, then it follows that sometimes our feelings may spring from sin rather than from legitimate needs.

If your husband voices a need that appears to be a cover for sin—like the pastor in our example who wants his wife to give him privacy online, despite his past porn use—then it's perfectly okay to call him on it. In fact, it's wrong to say nothing, because part of our responsibility as Christians is to help those around us live holy lives. James wrote,

> If one of you should wander from the truth and someone
> should bring that person back, remember this: Whoever
> turns a sinner from the error of their way will save them
> from death and cover over a multitude of sins.
> (James 5:19–20)

We are supposed to "bring them back" when we see them wandering from the truth. When we hear each other's unmet needs, then, it's perfectly okay to subject them to the sniff test: Does this smell right? Or is this a cover for something wrong?

In the case of this woman who was worried about her husband's porn use and who wanted full access to his computer, here's what I would suggest. He says that he has a need for privacy and that confession is between him and God alone (even though James 5:16 clearly states that we are to "confess your sins to each other"). She could say, "In marriage, we are one. There are no secrets. And if you are right with God, then you should have nothing to hide. If you aren't right with God, I need to know that so I can pray with you and support you."

If he still won't give her access, that's when the Matthew 18 admonition, which we talked about in Thought #6, should come into effect. If you have confronted your spouse and believe that he is still walking in sin, then it is time to bring someone else into the conversation to help you.

Action Step: If you believe your spouse is asking something unreasonable, seek counsel with one or two trusted people to help both of you gain proper perspective.

Sometimes, of course, that outside person may point out where you're in error! I remember speaking at a marriage conference when a quiet woman approached me about a problem she was having. She told me that her husband was verbally abusing their daughter. He often yelled and insisted that she meet very high standards. The mother's response was to go into the daughter's room and console her and tell her that her daddy didn't mean it and that she knew how upset this girl felt. This woman was driving a wedge between the father and the daughter, and her own marriage.

The woman then told me that she had brought it up numerous

times in her women's Bible study and even in their small group, asking for prayer for her husband to become more gentle, even with her husband sitting beside her.

As we talked about it, though, it became clear that the husband just wanted simple things: He wanted his daughter to actually do her chores. He wanted his daughter to practice piano and not to be on Facebook all the time. He wanted his daughter not to talk back to him. Yet if he raised his voice, his wife would intervene.

As conference speakers, we can't do counseling, because we only see couples for very brief times at these events. One thing I did suggest to this couple, though, was that they clarify the rules for their daughter and then discuss how to make sure those rules were followed. The wife was undermining her husband's role as a dad, and she was betraying him in front of their peers. Verbal abuse is real, but sometimes we call things abusive when they're simply not what we would do. And that's why it's often a good idea to get another opinion when you're at a crossroads and you both feel as if you are right and the other is wrong, or you wonder if something is crossing the threshold of abuse, addiction, or affairs.

I have had the opposite experience as well, listening, horrified, as a woman told me she was trying to submit to her husband but found it difficult when he would whip their eighteen-year-old son. I let her know very clearly that this was abusive—and pointed her and her kids to safety.

Sometimes you need someone to give you a reality check and tell you, "You're being unreasonable." Other times you need someone to do that to your husband. But isn't that what community is for? If you think your husband is arguing for something that is illegitimate and even sinful, that's when it's time to bring someone else in and ask for some help.

All of us will, at times, feel angry. If we take that anger first to God, and then focus on finding a win-win, we'll find that anger doesn't need to draw us apart. It can actually be a tool that God uses to help us have some hard, but very important, conversations, which speed us up on that quest to oneness.

Summary of Action Steps

1. Pray. Ask God to give you both wisdom as you work through this conflict.
2. Prepare. Identify your unmet needs and write them on a piece of paper (or share them with your spouse).
3. Problem solve. Brainstorm ways to meet your unmet needs and your spouse's unmet needs. Write it down, talk while walking, or sleep on it.
4. Learn. Determine each other's love languages and make a list of things that make each of you feel loved.
5. Seek outside help. If you believe your spouse's request is unreasonable or sinful, get someone you trust involved.

Thought #8

Having Sex Is Not the Same as Making Love

In May 1990 I started counting the days to my upcoming nuptials: 429. But it wasn't the wedding I was anticipating. It was the wedding *night*. I thought excitedly, *In just 429 days, the man I love is going to make me feel wonderful!* After years of trying to turn off my body, I'd be able to have sex any time I wanted. It never entered my head that sex wouldn't always be easy, or fun, or a romantic, intimate experience.

I'm sure most women have dreamed of that sort of rapturous sex life upon being married. We wanted to be swept off our feet; to be rendered breathless; to experience the fireworks. Sex seemed like such a beautiful promise.

Some may have discovered that bliss, but for many of us, reality failed to live up to the promise. We women want to be swept off our feet, but when our feet have indents from Polly Pockets and LEGOs, sleep often seems far more attractive than something gymnastic. We want to feel romantic, but when sex doesn't last long and doesn't always bring much pleasure, then we'd rather take our romance with a box of chocolates. And sure, we'd like to be breathless, but when he has gotten heavy—or when we've gotten heavy—we get breathless in all the wrong ways.

Sex loses its allure.

Our real life has collided with our expectations. We thought it would be passionate and rapturous, but it gets stale and boring. Yet I don't think lousy or mediocre sex is inevitable. I think we wind up with disappointment in the bedroom because most of us have never really understood the fundamental difference between sex and making love. Before I was married, I was mostly looking forward to sex itself; I didn't understand vulnerability and intimacy and mystery—the things that make sex profound. I really only understood arousal and orgasm, and I put a romantic spin on them. When my body didn't respond the way I wanted it to, though, sex seemed like too much work. Combine that with a culture that cheapens sex, and it's easy to see why many of us start to wonder what all the fuss is about.

OUR CULTURE MAKES SEX SEEM ICKY

Our culture has a weird relationship with sex. On the one hand we worship it, and on the other hand, we're actually having less sex today than couples did even two decades ago.[1]

Maybe that's because we've cheapened sex by forgetting that it's about more than just the body. Sex, marriage, and love were all supposed to be part and parcel of the same thing, yet today they're presented more like a buffet, where you can take what you want and leave behind the bacon bits if you choose. You can be in love without getting married; you can have sex without being in love—or without being married. You can even be married without sex!

When we take sex out of the context of a committed marriage relationship, we start down a dangerous path. God designed sex to be deeply intimate as well as physically pleasurable. If you're not committed to your partner, though, then sex can't be truly intimate. It's only about the body. And it's not even about your partner's body, since you'll likely change partners. The only constant in your sex life is *you*.

Thought #8:

Having sex is not the same as making love.

If you make sex all about the physical, then the only way to "improve" sex is to push the envelope. Try wild and exciting things. Explore your fantasies! Perhaps it's no wonder, then, that people end up feeling empty, used, and degraded. Instead of loving each other, people use each other.

MAKING LOVE REQUIRES INTIMACY

Right from the beginning, God made sex to be something intimate and beautiful, not just physical. A look at the Old Testament can show us that vividly.

I grew up in a church that used the King James Version of the Bible, and I distinctly remember hearing the pastor read from Genesis: "And Adam knew Eve his wife; and she conceived, and bare Cain" (Genesis 4:1, KJV). Back in those junior high days, we huddled in the pews, giggling and elbowing our friends with the hilarity. Instead of saying a word that meant "sex," the Bible used "knew." Obviously God was embarrassed at the actual word.

But hold on a second. What if something else was going on?

In Psalm 139, David said, "You have searched me, LORD, and you *know* me" (verse 1). And later he turned it into a prayer: "Search me, God, and *know* my heart" (verse 23). In fact, that theme, begging God to dig deep inside our hearts and really "know" us, is throughout Scripture. And the same Hebrew word—*yada,* or "to know"—is used to represent both our deep longing for a union with God and the sexual union between a husband and a wife.

What if there's actually a connection? What if sex isn't supposed to be just a physical union of genitalia, but is also intended to encompass this deep longing to be known?

That's part of God's plan for sex. Think about it: in sex we bare ourselves physically. But for sex to work well, especially for women, we also have to bare ourselves emotionally. We have to be vulnerable. We have to be willing to "let go."

As a marriage and sex blogger, I'm often inundated with e-mails from frustrated women asking, "Does God just have it in for women? Why is it so much easier for my husband to have a good time than it is for me to get aroused?" You, too, likely have noticed that your sexual response isn't nearly as automatic as your husband's. When I conducted surveys of two thousand people for my book *The Good Girl's Guide to Great Sex,* I found that the best years sexually for women were not the honeymoon days; they came instead a decade and a half later, after the couple had years to get comfortable with each other.[2] Those couples with the best sex lives were also more likely to rate their marriage as "spiritually intimate." When we feel close to each other, we respond better sexually.

I believe that God made us this way for a reason. For women to enjoy sex, we have to feel intimate. We have to choose to "let him in"—not just physically but emotionally—because it's all too easy just to look at ceiling tiles and ask yourself, "Is that smudge up there a spider?" And that's likely why orgasm isn't automatic for us.

Great sex, especially for women, requires communication. We need to tell our husbands what we like, and that can be difficult, since so many of us aren't even sure what we like or what we want! That's why great sex also takes vulnerability. We have to let our guard down so that we can figure out what we actually want. And then we need to trust him in order to tell him.

Communication, trust, and vulnerability are vital to a great sex life—but all of those things are also vital for a great marriage! If the sexual response were automatic, then we wouldn't have the same incentive to work on our friendship, to communicate, and to grow trust. This way, when things work well, we achieve true intimacy in all aspects of marriage—not just sex. But sex itself also feels stupendous because it isn't only physical. We're truly intimate. We're actually making love.

HOW MUCH DOES SEX MATTER IN A MARRIAGE?

Sex and intimacy are both vital components of making love, but for most of us, they're hard to achieve and prioritize. Take our culture that makes sex seem almost icky, and toss in the things many of us have dealt with from abuse to sexual harassment to growing up believing sex is shameful, and it's difficult to find intimacy. (If you struggle with some of these issues, see the appendix for resources that can help you overcome them.) Add exhaustion to the mix, along with the difficulty many of us have making sex pleasurable, and making love seems like too much work. With all of these forces working against us, perhaps it's not surprising that in my surveys, 44 percent of couples reported having sex less than once a week.[3]

Our church culture has noticed this frequency crisis and has grown alarmed by it. Leaders have decided to rectify the problem by advocating sex, sex, and more sex.

Pat Answer: *Just do it! Men need sex frequently, so women need to give it to them!*

Book series have been written about the battles that men face with sexual temptation, and wives are told that they can help men defeat these temptations by having sex more often. Some pastors challenge couples to have sex every day (in some cases for a week, and in some cases, for a month) to reap the benefits in their marriage.[4]

I have sympathy with this approach. On a spiritual level, every time you make love, you reaffirm your relationship and you feel more committed. And from a practical standpoint, libido in women is largely a use-it-or-lose-it phenomenon. When we have sex more frequently, our bodies tend to respond more easily, and we'll find that our libidos increase. When women have sex less frequently, our bodies often shut down and our desire for sex diminishes.

Also, remember my story of "sex flowers" from Thought #1? My husband felt close to me after making love, and so he brought me flowers. That's how God designed us. When we experience sexual release, we release the bonding hormone oxytocin, which helps us feel closer to each other. When we're making love with relative frequency, we tend to feel more positively toward each other, and we tend to find it easier to let go of small issues in the marriage.

These are all good things, yet simply having more sex will not make everything automatically better. Our religious "just do it" pat answer seems too much like a mirror image of our culture's attitude toward sex: both ignore the fact that sex is more than genitalia. It isn't a cure-all for everything, and too often it's portrayed as such. That cheapens sex too.

Making love—experiencing genuine intimacy through sex—is truly beautiful. But too many couples haven't experienced that because they've bought into this "sex is only about genitalia," sometimes without even realizing it. So let's look at the problems with seeing sex as a cure-all for everything.

Problem #1: We Make Sex Sound as If It's Just for Men

If you tell women, "Men really, truly need sex. Never say no, or you're hurting him, and he could end up having an affair"—who is going to be turned on by that?

God designed sex to be a mutually satisfying experience. *Both* of us are supposed to enjoy it. It's supposed to make *both* of us feel more intimate. *Both* of us need it. The only real difference is that men, in general, feel more of an urgent physical need for it. But the best way to meet that need is to realize that we have a need for it too, and then to act on it. If we hear this message that men "need" sex and we women therefore must perform, it's all too easy to start seeing sex as distasteful and men as animals. We may think, *God must care about my husband more than me. God made me as a receptacle for my husband to use.* That is *not* what God intended at all.

Instead of emphasizing his need for sex, then, let's emphasize mutually satisfying sex—something that you both want, that you both find pleasurable, and that you both find intimate. And sex does have great benefits for us! It can feel wonderful. It relieves stress. It wards off depression, viruses, and migraines. It even helps us sleep better! So many times I turned my husband down because I was just too exhausted. Yet those nights when I said no I could never sleep well. I always felt as if there was something between us. When we make love, though, I fall asleep almost immediately and sleep really deeply. So now, when I'm super tired, I turn to Keith and say, "Come put me to sleep, baby!"

Let's stop talking about sex as something that men need and that women need to give, and start talking about sex as something that is wonderful for both of us, together. That's the message Paul gave in 1 Corinthians 7: the wife's body belongs to the husband, but the husband's body also belongs to the wife. Making love is supposed to be about mutuality. When we frame it primarily in terms of one person's needs, then we're no longer making love. We're just having sex. And that can feel really shallow.

Action Step: Hold a "sexual check-in" with each other. Start the discussion by listing all the things you both like about sex.

Then ask each other: "How do you feel about our frequency? our passion? our pleasure? Where can we improve?"

Problem #2: Men Want to Be Wanted, Not Placated

The "just say yes" advice plants another potential land mine. It implies that what men need is sexual release and it ignores the fact that men crave real intimacy too.

After spending several of the first years of our marriage pulling out flannel nightgowns to turn Keith off, I had an epiphany. I would try the opposite approach! I would become the Most Amazing Wife ever and I would never, ever say no.

And I did. For several weeks I never turned him down, not even once.

Then he came to me one day, disheartened, and said, "I just feel like we never make love."

Those were fighting words. There I was, sacrificing so much so he'd finally stop bugging me, and he was still whining. So I pulled out a calendar and started circling all the days that we had sex. The next time he said, "I just feel like we never make love," I pulled out that calendar and told him, "You have nothing to complain about, buddy!"

After a rather heated conversation that night, it finally hit me. Keith didn't want to be placated; he wanted to be wanted. Women often dismiss how much men need to feel they can give pleasure to their wives. Men cannot have sex if they are not aroused; physically it just doesn't work. Women, however, can have sex and create a grocery list in their heads all at the same time, and men know this. The only way to tell if a woman really wants him is to see if she responds to him. Is she making love? Or is she just letting him have sex?

That feels like such a tall order for us, though. Not only do I have to do it, but I have to *want* to as well? Doesn't that mean that my feelings don't matter?

It can seem that way, but I don't think so. A woman's sex drive is almost entirely in her brain. A guy's is a little lower, but a woman's rests mostly in what she thinks. When she thinks positively about sex, then sex tends to be exciting. When she isn't really into it, sex often doesn't work very well.

Think about it this way: one night your husband can do something that has you in raptures, while the next night he's doing exactly the same thing, but you're lying there thinking, *Will you just get it over with because I want to get to sleep.* It's not what he's doing; it's all about *your attitude* toward what he's doing.

We women don't always understand this about ourselves. We think that our libidos work the same as men's, and that we should get in the mood first. And so we figure that before we make love we should be panting and aroused and excited. However, for the majority of women, arousal only kicks in after making love starts. When we decide, *I'm going to feel good tonight!* and then we jump him, our bodies usually follow. By flipping that mental switch, we're telling our husbands, *I do want to experience this with you. I do want to feel one with you.* And that's what he really craves.

Action Step: Initiate sex once a week. You can make love more often, but once a week, make sure you're the initiator!

Problem #3: Pornography Has Made Intimacy Almost Impossible
Pornography has taken all the mystery out of sex by making it stark, graphic, and perverse. As one recovering porn user said in a TED talk, "Porn doesn't even use hands."[5] The "mystery" part of sex—the part that unites us and makes us feel like one—is taken out and replaced by something impersonal.

And when that happens, whether it's the husband or the wife who uses porn (since 30 percent of porn addicts are now female),[6] the "just do it" solution won't help, because our whole sexual arousal process has been rewired. We were designed to be aroused in relationship, with love being a key ingredient that boosts sexual response. When arousal and sexual release are paired with pornographic images, though, our brains start to make a connection between sexual arousal and those images. Then it becomes difficult to be aroused by a real person. Italian researchers have found that porn has very destructive effects, especially for men: "Over time, [porn use] can lead to a loss of libido, impotence and a notion of sex that is totally divorced from real-life relations."[7] Reading erotica can have similar effects on women. Arousal becomes paired with fantasy rather than relationship, and then sexual response with an actual person is seriously hindered.

If sex is going to be something that helps us "know" each other and be intimate, then it's not only about increasing the frequency. It's also about eliminating counterfeit methods of sexual arousal like pornography or erotica.

REDISCOVERING GODLY SEXUALITY

I have known what it is to have a lousy sex life, and I have known what it is to have a great sex life. And the great one is so much better! Even if sex is a stumbling block in your marriage, you can discover what God wants for you: a beautiful sex life with your husband that's mutually satisfying, that's intimate, and that rocks your world. Here's how:

If He's Got a Low Libido, Figure Out Why

According to the survey I did, 23 percent of the women who will read this book have a higher libido than their husbands.[8] We normally think that all men want sex and all women need to be convinced, so if you're in a marriage where you're hot and bothered and he'd rather sleep, the dejection is even worse. Add our religious culture's admonition to "just do it," and it's like pouring lemon juice on a thousand paper cuts.

Every marriage has libido differences, and if you simply want sex more often than he does, that may not be a big problem. However, if your husband rarely if ever wants sex, it's worth figuring out why his libido has plummeted.

A guy's low libido usually falls into one of these categories: he has low testosterone; he has other medical issues affecting libido; he has suffered sexual dysfunction in the past and is now nervous about sex; he is stressed for other reasons; he has experienced trauma in his past, including sexual abuse; or he's obtaining sexual release elsewhere, such as through porn and masturbation. Make sure low libido or sexual dysfunction are not rooted in medical conditions, because often these are fixable, and many medical causes could be an early warning sign of something else. If the issue is stress, talk to him about how you can help him fight it. And if it's past trauma, ask him to seek out a trained counselor. God doesn't want our pasts hindering our marriages today.

For most men today, though, low libido (and often the accompanying sexual dysfunction, like erectile dysfunction or premature ejaculation) is caused by porn use.[9]

Confront Sexual Sin

If your husband is involved with pornography, making love to him more often or acting like a porn star will not stop the addiction. Your husband has rewired his brain to become aroused to an image rather than a person, and that chemical reaction has to be attacked before you can experience true intimacy during sex. Few men can defeat the lure of porn without an accountability partner. Using the steps outlined in some of the previous chapters about confronting sin, talk to your husband, set boundaries, and above all, do not put up with porn in your marriage. Some specific resources are listed in the appendix to help you and your husband work through this.

If you are the one struggling with porn use or with reading erotic materials, confess your struggles to your husband. Although it may feel humiliating, you can't achieve real intimacy if you're holding back. Jennifer Smith, aka *The Unveiled Wife* blogger, had her share of problems galore with sex when she first married—pain, embarrassment, rejection. Slowly, one by one, God dealt with each of the issues. But there was one area that Jennifer would rather have left in the dark: her own porn use. She and her husband had addressed his porn use, but she'd never opened up about her own. The thought of doing so seemed mortifying.

When she finally confessed, though, she and her husband experienced a level of spiritual intimacy they had never encountered before. Jennifer wasn't holding anything back; she was completely baring her soul to her husband. And through that one act, God started the major healing process both in their hearts and in the bedroom.

By keeping the secret, we think we're sparing ourselves embarrassment and sparing our husbands hurt, but often we're just cheating ourselves of real intimacy. Confess to someone and stop hiding, and you will find healing comes much more quickly.

Action Step: Deal with any sexual sin in your marriage, whether his or yours. Make sure that porn or erotica have no place in your relationship. Arrange accountability for whoever has the problem.

Address Physical Issues

If sex hurts, hearing "just do it" is a terrible message. While for most women sex is pleasurable, about 12 percent find sex painful. Between 1 and 6 percent of women suffer from full-blown vaginismus,[10] a condition where the muscles of the vagina tense up so that intercourse is virtually impossible. Treatments are available that can help you learn how to relax the muscles, and as you feel more confident in your marriage, the condition does usually subside.

Jennifer Smith's problems with sex started out as physical: she couldn't have sex for the first four years of her marriage due to extreme dryness and pain. After researching it on the Internet, she and her husband discovered that she had an extreme sensitivity to parabens, the preservatives found in most cosmetics, body washes, and shampoos. "When I switched my products I felt different within three days and experienced pain-free sex in a matter of weeks," Jennifer wrote.[11]

Our bodies are complex systems; stress and fear can cause us to tense up, but so can environmental causes. The bottom line: if this is a problem for you, do research and get some help! Don't settle for pain.

Other women face different physical challenges, from general chronic pain to multiple sclerosis or fibromyalgia. Again, the message "he needs you to have sex," when sex hurts, sounds as though God is heartless.

Enlarge your view of sex so that it isn't just intercourse, but it's also about relaxation. Start with a bath. Make massage an integral part of sex. Prioritize orgasm, even if it's through manual or oral stimulation. Sexual release can be a great pain reliever. And then seek help to get to the root of your issue, because for most women, pain during sex is certainly treatable, if not curable.

Make Sex Pleasurable

If you're one of the roughly 40 percent of married women who rarely or never achieve orgasm with intercourse,[12] then hearing "just do it" can be humiliating too. So how about another message? God created women to experience great sexual pleasure. He even gave us a piece of anatomy—the clitoris—which has only one purpose, to arouse us. When we do reach climax, that climax can be much deeper and more intense than a man's. If you've never experienced that, you can. It just may take some work.

That's what my friend Rajdeep found with her husband. Roiling with frustration after being married for a year, she had never experienced "The Big O." Then a wise mentor told her to take her time. They had been rushing things, putting too much pressure on getting to The Big Event. But when they persevered and didn't give up, they finally got the results they wanted.[13]

Experiencing that awesome feeling during intercourse can take some women even longer. Part of the problem is that, like Rajdeep, we work ourselves up so much that we can't relax. For orgasm to happen, you have to give in to the pleasure rather than trying to force it. That takes time to learn—and it takes time and trust to completely relax.

But you can get there! Turn sex into a great research project that you and your husband can do together. Buy Christian books on how to make sex feel wonderful for you (some are listed in the appendix). For many women it takes a number of years to figure out this whole sex thing, but that span can be shortened if you learn more about your sexuality, if you work on your friendship so you're not as embarrassed, and if you take your time!

Action Step: Ask your husband to do an exciting research
project with you—figuring out how to make sex feel great!
Pick a few books from the appendix and start exploring.

Address Emotional Issues

Often the reason we balk when people tell us to "just do it,"
though, is that things in our past have made sex seem really ugly.
How can something so gross and even abusive be the way that
God wants my husband to experience love? It seems almost cruel.
Author Mary DeMuth has been candid about how her past sexual
abuse made being this "sexy wife" that we hear about nearly impossible. Her abuse, she said, "made me think that my sole purpose in this life was to be used and violated."[14] She's learned how
to focus on intimacy, but the abuse still holds her back, and she
has to fight to stop from disconnecting.

One of my readers, Ashleigh, grew up in a house where the
purity culture was preached so much that sex seemed evil—and
her body was deemed a temptation to men, so she became ashamed
of it. These childhood messages about sex, learned either through
abuse or through poor teaching on our parents' part, can make it
difficult even to understand the concept of "making love." The
physical act seems so far from loving. If you're walking through
this, please seek out a counselor to talk through your issues with.
God doesn't want you stuck.

Other women find that past emotional issues aren't the problem; current ones conspire to make sex the last thing on our minds.
My friend Cheri, whose story I told you in Thought #4, and who's

married to her own version of Spock (or Sheldon), found that "just do it" was a horrible message to close the gulf between her and her husband, because it associated stern personal discipline with sex. For a woman whose deep need for emotional connection wasn't being met, telling her to "just do it" felt overwhelming.

I understand, because I was there too. One of the things I loved most about my husband when we were dating was that we could sit for hours and just talk—about important stuff, about not so important stuff, about anything. When we got married, I believed that's what intimacy was—the ability to talk about anything and still feel as if the other person heard you. But somehow over the course of the first few years of our marriage we lost that. When we'd have a particularly bad few weeks, I would think back to those dating days and wish that I could get back to "real intimacy." If only we could just talk for hours again, we'd feel close.

I now realize that I was wrong.

Talking and sharing your heart is a wonderful part of intimacy, but it is only a part. And in marriage, it isn't enough. When we don't make love, or when we make love only rarely, intimacy in our marriage is hindered.

Intimacy is about sharing something with your spouse that you don't share with anybody else. It's letting him in. It's laughing together. And it's also feeling that deep hunger for each other. Somewhat ironically, when you feel that way, you're often more drawn to pray together, because you've already become vulnerable with each other. You've let down all the pretenses. That's also why when you pray together first, sex is even more intense.

Often we women think that we need to feel emotionally close before we can have a great sex life. That's natural, because in general, women need to feel loved to want to make love. But may I make a suggestion? Understand that it works the other way for him: *men need to make love to feel loved*. And if you concentrate on loving him that way and becoming more vulnerable and more selfless, it's likely that he'll also feel closer to you in other areas of your marriage too.

That's what Cheri found. When she started to understand that sex was how her Spock experienced love, and it was a gift that she could give him, she found that she felt closer to him too. It wasn't just that he was happier; it was that she felt more connected. And then it was easier to work on the problems they were having with emotional connection outside of the bedroom.

The same worked for my marriage. When I started prioritizing sex, I suddenly got my best friend back again.

Some things we do need to sort out before we can just "jump in," like sexual sin, physical problems, or past sexual trauma. But emotional distance isn't one of them. It's like the chicken and the egg: Which comes first, the sex or the friendship? It's hard to disentangle them. If you have a deep need for friendship, you'll likely find that it's easier to achieve if you also put a priority on sex.

If you've been diminishing the importance of sex in your marriage because you feel distant or it feels like too much work, maybe you need to hear a man's perspective. Here's a comment that was recently left on my blog by a man whose wife consents to sex only about once a month:

There is little to no romance anymore, which is not to say there is no love, friendship, or mutual respect. She likes sex. It feels good. But in contrast to my view of the act as a bonding, meaningful expression of love and devotion, to her it's "just sex."

Over the years I've hit all the bases, emotionally trying to understand her point of view. But the problem is—and I don't think many women really ever understand this—after a while all that rejection builds up, and to protect ourselves we have to lose interest in sex ourselves or go mad. Sports takes on greater meaning, as does a drink with the boys at the bar, or a book or newspaper.

I love my wife. And overall we have a good relationship. But to be honest, it's amazing how interest in a spouse wanes once sex is off the table.

LEARN TO "MAKE LOVE"

Everything we've been talking about leads up to this last point: spiritual intimacy through sex is a beautiful thing. I'm not talking about something out of the Kama Sutra or some eastern religion. I'm talking about that deep hunger to connect that is part of sex—not just a desire for orgasm, but a desire to be joined. How, practically, can we experience "spiritual intimacy" so that sex is more than sex—it's actually making love?

Action Step: At least once a month, make sex into a romantic, intimate experience instead of just a pleasurable one. Put it in your calendar! Use candles. Give each other massages first. And using the steps below, make sex into something that says "I love you," not just "I need you."

1. Spend Time Naked

Hold each other. Take a bath together. Even pray naked together! Touch each other's body. It's actually more vulnerable to be naked while someone touches you than just to be naked while you "have sex." When you're able to be vulnerable, sex becomes more personal.

2. Be Spiritually Naked

This may sound weird, but pray before sex—or at least read a psalm or something! When we unite together spiritually first, our souls are drawn together. And when our souls are drawn together, we want to draw together in a deeper way.

3. Look into Each Other's Eyes

The eyes are windows to the soul, and yet how often do we close our eyes, as if we're trying to shut out the other person and concentrate on ourselves? I know sometimes you have to close your eyes to feel everything, but occasionally open up. To actually see him—and to let him see into you—is very intimate, especially at the height of passion.

4. Say "I Love You"

While you're making love, or even when you orgasm, say "I love you." Make sex not just about feeling good but about expressing love. Say his name. Show him that you're thinking of him in particular.

5. Feed Your Desire for Your Spouse

Spiritual intimacy during sex ultimately depends on that desire to be united with your spouse. And that desire is fed throughout the day—by concentrating on what you love about him, by thinking about him, by flirting and playing with him, by saying positive things about him to others. It isn't something that "just happens." It's the culmination of the relationship you already have.

6. Laugh.

One of the most intimate things is sharing an inside joke. And sometimes we take sex far too seriously! When you can run upstairs and play "beat the clock" for a quickie while the kids are entertained by a video, you'll giggle throughout the rest of the evening. Having this fun part of your life that only the two of you see is intimate in and of itself. So don't be afraid to giggle, explore, and just enjoy each other.

Many of us push sex out of the way because it seems like a chore, but in doing so we deny ourselves one of the most powerful tools we have to feel truly connected and accepted by our spouse.

If sex makes you feel dirty or is a constant source of conflict, then pray through past issues and put them to rest. But if it's simply that you've never experienced making love this way, then try those steps. Concentrate on what you love about each other. Pray together. Memorize each other's bodies. Say "I love you." Look into each other's eyes. Truly be joined.

For the first four years of her marriage, Jennifer Smith doubted if she and her husband could ever have sex, since her intense pain had kept them from engaging fully in intercourse. They tried to do other sexual things, but Jennifer constantly felt like a failure, and so any kind of sexual activity became sporadic.

When the breakthrough finally came, and the pain vanished, making love still wasn't automatic. "I still anticipated the pain, so it was hard to see sex as an intimate thing," Jennifer explained to me. Gradually, as she started to understand how much her husband felt loved through sex, she began to see it as a positive act—though still mostly for him. It didn't become intimate for her as well until she made the mind-shift to believe, *I can initiate too. I don't have to just respond and wait for him. I can start this whole thing and get excited about it!* When she started to initiate, she got her head in the game. She wasn't waiting for something to happen; *she* was making it happen. And it worked!

I asked Jennifer what sex was like now compared with those four years when they were struggling, or even those initial first few encounters. She laughed and replied, "Oh, there's no comparison. It's a 180-degree turn. I finally know what intimacy is!" She has learned to make love, and now they really feel like they're one.

Summary of Action Steps

1. Run through a sexual check-in with your husband. Figure out what you like best and what you need to work on.
2. Initiate sex once a week.
3. Confront sexual sin, and arrange for accountability if one or both of you struggle with porn or erotica.
4. Start a research project to figure out how to bring you both the most pleasure. Read books and spend time exploring.
5. Once a month, schedule a more romantic, intimate, and intense lovemaking session, focusing on saying "I love you," not just "I want you."

Thought #9

If I'm Not Careful, We'll Drift Apart

Sea otters sleep holding hands—or holding paws is perhaps more exact. It ranks up there as one of the most adorable things in nature, just slightly under YouTube videos of babies tasting lemons.

And why do otters do something so over the top with cuteness? That way, while they're sleeping, they can't drift apart. Sea otters know that currents can cause them to drift, and if they're going to move, they want to make sure their loved ones move with them.

That's a pretty smart mammal, because drifting is a very real danger. I read once of an experiment in which researchers dropped a number of "messages in bottles" into the water off the coast of Brazil, complete with notes detailing how to claim a reward if you contacted them once you found the bottle. One bottle washed up on the coast of Nicaragua about one hundred days later. Another bottle took roughly a year to travel in the opposite direction across the Atlantic Ocean and around the Cape of Good Hope, finally depositing itself in Tanzania, on the east coast of Africa.

Thought #9:

If I'm not careful, we'll drift apart.

The bottles started in exactly the same spot, but they ended up half a world away from each other.

The natural pull in life is to drift apart. Currents are carrying us away—currents we often don't even see. None of us gets married thinking we'll end up half a world apart, yet if we aren't intentional like those sea otters, we very likely will wake up one day, look at our spouse, and think, *Who are you?*

WHAT CAN STOP THE DRIFT?

I've attended so many weddings I've lost count. My husband has a big family, and we have a large circle of church friends, so it seems as though every May and June I'm busy buying cards and finding dresses and heading off to another lovely nuptial.

When witnessing all of these weddings, I've only once ever thought, *They'll divorce in less than ten years.* (Unfortunately, I was right.) All the couples looked so in love. And yet about 20 percent of Christian marriages will end in divorce. Now that's not nearly as high as we may think; Shaunti Feldhahn ran the actual census numbers in her book *The Good News About Marriage* and concluded that the incidence of divorce has been highly exaggerated.[1] Nevertheless, it's still a lot of heartache.

How does a relationship with such promise turn into a disaster?

The couple stops being intentional. We've talked about how oneness is the goal of marriage, but oneness is not automatic. In the last thought we looked at how to stay intentional with physical intimacy. Here let's look at how to stay intentional with our spiritual and emotional intimacy.

Being Intentional: Spiritual Intimacy

Sixteenth-century philosopher Blaise Pascal argued, in essence, that we are all created with a "God-shaped vacuum" that can only be filled by our creator.[2] We long for intimacy and acceptance and love, but that longing can be met completely only by God, not by our mate. That's probably why Shaunti Feldhahn's research found that Christian couples were happier: 53 percent of highly happy couples looked to God for their fulfillment, not their spouse, compared with just 7 percent of struggling couples.[3] Our longing for intimacy with God is our most fundamental desire.

Unfortunately, for many couples, spiritual intimacy is not always so easily attained. Remember the story I told in Thought #5 of my reader who felt her outdoorsy husband wasn't a spiritual leader because he didn't lead their family in devotions? In their case, spirituality was pulling them apart.

Gary Thomas, in his book *Sacred Pathways,* suggests another way to look at how we worship and how we can connect spiritually. He posits that there are nine different spiritual temperaments, or preferences, to relate to God and to nourish one's soul.[4] One pathway isn't necessarily better or worse; it's just different. My reader's husband relates to God in nature and through service. She relates to God with colored pencils, prayer journals, and highlighters. The church tends to praise her intellectual way and make it sound as if it is the "right" way, yet both she and her husband share a yearning for God—they just express it differently. Her life verse may be, "Your word is a lamp for my feet, a light on my path" (Psalm 119:105), while his may be, "As the deer pants for streams of water, so my soul pants for you, my God" (Psalm 42:1).

All of the nine spiritual pathways can be found throughout Scripture and church history, but we tend to pull out just a few favorites and portray them as the "right" way of doing spirituality within our families. That can backfire, because if we tend more toward the prayer and Bible-reading side—or even if we don't, but we expect our husbands to—we send them the message, *You're not spiritual enough.* And that can accelerate the drift.

I sometimes look at my friend with that nature-loving husband and wonder why she doesn't see what the rest of us do: a superinvolved dad who gives of his time in order to get to know his kids and their friends. What would happen if she stopped feeling bitter that they don't do family devotions and every day she started saying, "Isn't it great how they see you loving God's creation! Your enthusiasm is contagious!"?

Action Step: Study your husband and figure out his spiritual bent. Then validate it and acknowledge it.

Pray Together

Even if your husband does have a different sacred pathway, you can pray together. Prayer stops the drift between the two of you, and prayer is powerful. For many of us, though, praying out loud ranks with public speaking as one of the scariest things to do. John and Stasi Eldredge described praying together like this: "Prayer is such an intimate act, a place of vulnerability. It is, hopefully, when we are our least guarded, our most honest selves."[5] That kind of vulnerability can be intimidating, but it's also the doorway to a deep and abiding spiritual intimacy. Too many couples don't experience this though, because they don't pray together at all.

How can we make prayer less intimidating?

Start by asking your husband if you can pray for something specific with him. Saying "Can we pray together" is more intimidating than "Can we take a moment and pray about Johnny's bullying situation at school?" The former sounds like anything from "I want to pray for two hours on my knees with you" to "I want to pray that our awful, horrible marriage will completely turn around." He may not know what to make of it. So start with something specific, with boundaries around the request.

When you do pray about that specific thing, stick to it. If your husband isn't comfortable praying out loud, then don't embellish too much yourself. Pray at the level of the one who is least comfortable. Take to heart this practical admonition from Solomon: "Do not be quick with your mouth, do not be hasty in your heart to utter anything before God. God is in heaven and you are on earth, so let your words be few" (Ecclesiastes 5:2).

If praying out loud is still too intimidating, what about using prewritten prayers? For a time our family attended an Anglican church, and I discovered that the prayer book prayers are truly beautiful. We attend a more evangelical church now, but both Keith and I miss the depth of the Anglican prayers. (In Gary Thomas's language, both Keith and I share a sacred pathway that's rooted in traditional liturgy.) So we purchased a few books of prayers and every so often we pray through them as a family, especially when we're camping together. We have a book of Celtic prayers we love, and there's just something about an Irish prayer in the great outdoors that works!

Your spiritual life should be something that keeps you together, like holding paws, not a current that drives you apart. But which one it is will depend upon your attitude. Are you approaching your husband with the expectation that he'll behave in a certain stereotypical way, or are you leaving room for God to do something that may be outside the mainstream?

Action Step: Make prayer a regular part of your marriage— even if it's just a few sentences at a time, or even if the prayers are prewritten ones.

BEING INTENTIONAL: EMOTIONAL INTIMACY

One night he staggers home from work, exhausted, and instead of eating at the table with her, he grabs dinner, puts his feet up, and watches TV. She's tired too, so after the kids go to bed she retreats into the study to surf Pinterest. A few more times that week they re-create the scene, and soon it becomes the evening routine. Once couples stop communicating, laughing, and sharing, then the only thing that binds them together is the children. And eventually children aren't enough. The drift has grown too wide.

The only way to stop the drift is to be deliberate. Laziness isn't an option. In Proverbs 10:4, Solomon wrote, "Lazy hands make for poverty, but diligent hands bring wealth." Solomon may have been talking about laziness in regards to work and money, but the same principle is true for relationships. If we want riches in our marriage, we can't be lazy.

Brad Wilcox from the University of Virginia has studied happily married couples extensively, and he found that 83 percent of highly happy couples spend at least thirty minutes per week in some activity together, compared with just 35 percent of struggling couples.[6] But it isn't that happy people tend to hang out more; it's that people who hang out more are happy! Just being together tends to increase happiness. When couples have tension, though, we naturally want to pull apart and spend less time together. Big mistake, says Shaunti Feldhahn.[7] In her research, she found that when stressed couples spend more time together rather than less, the stress tends to go away.

Check In with Your Spouse

My aunt and uncle have been married forty-three years. No couple spends more time doing stuff together than they do—they even worked together at their own home business for several decades! They canoe, they bike, they attend Irish-dancing ceilidhs. But this year they began a new daily "check in" exercise, which made them feel even more emotionally close. At the end of the day, they both sit in their comfy chairs by the fire, with candlelight, and share their "consolation" and their "desolation" of the day.

Based on Ignatius's writings,[8] they talk about what was life affirming that day (their consolation) and what they felt sucked life away (their desolation). Some people have called this exercise their "highs" and "lows," but they prefer to think about not just what makes them happy or sad, but what actually energizes or not, because sometimes these are different things. The rules: there are no right or wrong answers, and you can't criticize each other. You just listen and learn.

You'd think that a couple who've already spent so much time together wouldn't need this, but my aunt has found that by having to share her day, she has to analyze it. She has to answer the question herself. And as they share their desolations especially, they can observe patterns. They're learning more about what makes each other tick—even after more than forty years together.

Keith and I started this exercise during our recent busy seasons too. We've noticed that while we have always talked a lot, we haven't always been deliberate about going deep and sharing about our vulnerabilities and fears. Because of that intentional choice to check in with each other, now even if we're apart for several days, we can Skype or talk daily and still know how the other is doing emotionally. We check in not just about what we've done that day, but about how we've felt and what has thrown us through a loop or what has brought us peace. Besides staying connected with Keith, those times have become opportunities for me to learn more about myself too!

> **Action Step:** Every day take five minutes and share your "consolation" and "desolation." If you'd like, use a candle to make the time more special.

Grow Your Friendship

Friendship in marriage is the glue that keeps you together. When you're friends, you build up positive goodwill. That goodwill is like a deposit you make into a relationship bank account. What's unique about a relationship account, though, is that it can't go into overdraft. If you're going to make a withdrawal—by, for instance, bringing up a difficult issue—then you need to have a balance in there first.

Some of us were in the habit of building goodwill when we were dating, because we figured out things to do and we liked hanging out together. But after the wedding when life became busy, we settled into routines that included much less time together. Others of us never really were friends, even before we married. We loved each other, but we never really *did* anything together. Our dating life consisted mostly of watching movies or making out. How do you build a friendship with your husband now, even if you don't have a history of doing things together?

Think side-by-side, not face-to-face.

When women picture spending time together, we often picture face-to-face encounters. If we want to share our hearts with our husbands, we want to sit down over coffee, eyeball to eyeball, and talk about our day. But if you were to say to your husband, "I want to spend fifteen minutes of the day just talking to you," he'd likely get nervous. Is he in trouble?

Men, in general, tend to communicate side by side, when they're doing something together. Women like to communicate face to face. But communication happens either way! So instead of saying, "I want to spend fifteen minutes talking," why not say, "Can we take a walk after dinner every night to get a little exercise and fresh air?" The effect is the same—fifteen minutes of talking—but it's a different dynamic.

I mention this concept quite a bit on my blog, and recently a young mom e-mailed me to report that this simple ritual had turned her marriage around. It was such a small thing, but putting the kids in strollers and going for a walk every night let her and her husband connect, and she stopped brooding about how he never talked to her. They caught up, they laughed, and they felt connected again.

Action Step: Brainstorm ways to spend time side by side together weekly. Go for a walk, play a sport, explore a new area, fix up the house, do a puzzle. Do something—anything! Then schedule it regularly.

Megan, a friend whose sons are all involved in hockey, found that identifying a simple way of spending time with her husband,

Doug, improved their marriage dramatically too. She noticed that she and her husband were feeling more and more distant because they didn't have much time together. They were taking turns driving the kids to practice and to games, so they each could have time for themselves throughout the week. But Megan started to realize she needed time with Doug more than she needed time by herself, so she started tagging along with Doug on Doug's days. Twenty minutes in the car there, an hour and a half on a cold bench at the rink, and twenty minutes in the car home. That's a lot of time doing nothing together, time when they could just catch up.

Duke Vipperman, a pastor friend of mine building up an inner-city Toronto church, has concluded that "true community comes only when you can waste time together."[9] Just being together, even if there's no agenda, can reap major benefits. And couples who spend time together, even if they're not doing much of anything, will rarely drift.

BEING INTENTIONAL: PUTTING THE MARRIAGE BEFORE THE KIDS

Are you a better wife or a better mother?

I ask that question frequently when I speak, and "better mother" always wins. As soon as our kids are born, it is as if our hearts are walking around outside our chests. We love them so much, and we don't want to mess them up. And they're fragile! Our husbands, who are adults, should be able to fend for themselves, shouldn't they? The kids need us more.

Cultural Message: *Your kids are kids—they need you. Your husband is an adult; he can take care of himself.*

That's a common sentiment. And I think it's wrong.

You cannot be a good mother unless you are first a good wife, because the best gift you can give your children is to love their father. Children from a stable home where parents love each other are more likely to have healthy relationships themselves. They are less likely to use alcohol or drugs as teens. They are less likely to get pregnant before they're married. They're more likely to finish school. They're more likely to hold down a decent job. They're less likely to commit crimes. They're even less likely to be obese! And they are far more likely to be happy and emotionally secure.[10]

If we say no to our children in favor of their dad, it feels wrong, as if we are somehow being selfish. But we're not. *We're giving our kids a gift.*

If you spend your life chauffeuring your kids to extracurricular activities but have no time or energy to spend time talking with your husband every night, you may be sacrificing wifehood for motherhood. Your kids don't need to be involved in every activity, even if they're gifted at something. They need a solid family.

If you spend all your energy on your kids and never take any time to yourself so that you're exhausted by the end of the day, you're giving your best to your kids instead of to your husband. Your children will survive watching a video or two so you can put your feet up during the day and read a book or relax, to help you get in the right frame of mind later.

If you spend hours trying to get the kids to settle into bed or if you lie down with them yourself (or put them to sleep in *your* bed) and end up spending the evening with them, rather than with your husband, you may have a problem.

You need time with your husband, even if that means your children don't have all your attention. Sure, your kids may whine and cry, but *they are children.* They are, by nature, self-absorbed, and they do not know what is best for them. They aren't mature enough to realize that what they really want is two parents who love each other. Pray through the question: *Am I sacrificing my marriage for my kids?* Ultimately, your children don't want you to. Do not let your kids become a current that drives you apart.

Action Step: Ask your husband, "Do I neglect you in favor of the kids?" Talk about ways you can lessen the kids' demands on your energy and your time. Agree on one thing you will stop doing with the kids and one thing you will start doing with your husband.

BEING INTENTIONAL: GO TO SLEEP TOGETHER

I want to end the book with one more action step that is relatively simple, but that can make the biggest difference in our marriages: go to bed at the same time. Just like those otters, closing their eyes and holding their paws, we need to turn in together too.

Over the last few years I have talked to thousands of couples at marriage conferences and at events, and I keep hearing stories about how "we never talk" or "we never do anything together" or even, "our sex life is almost nonexistent." And when I start probing, I often find a similar story: "We don't go to bed at the same time."

I would venture to say that in most homes today, after dinner is over, various family members scatter to their own screens—either the computer or the TV or the video game system. And eventually somebody gets tired and heads to bed, but the other person doesn't join them for several hours.

And we wonder why we feel disconnected.

When reading the *Little House on the Prairie* series of books with my kids, one thing that always struck me was how early everyone woke up. Pa was up before the sun to get the farm ready for the day. But the reason he was able to get up that early without an alarm was that he went to bed with the sun.

With the advent of electricity, we started staying up later, because we could still be productive even after the sun went down. But I remember as a child that most people still went to bed at 11:00. The reason was simple: all the good TV shows ended at 11:00. Yet just as electricity pushed bedtimes back, now computers have virtually eliminated them altogether. With the Internet and video games you can do the exact same thing at 1:30 in the morning as you can at 8:00 in the evening. Our electronics suck us in.

How can we keep a marriage alive if we scatter at night? Keith and I spend a lot of time just chatting in bed—or even chatting while getting ready for bed. It's an important ritual, to spend the last few moments of the day holding each other. And I'm not just talking about sex. Sure, it's going to be harder to connect sexually if you're not in bed at the same time. But it's also harder to connect *at all*.

> **Action Step:** Figure out what time you need to get up in the morning, and count backward from that. If you need eight and a half hours of sleep, and you have to get up at 6:30, then you need to be going to sleep by 10:00 and going to bed at 9:30.

I know it's not possible for couples to turn in together when shift work is involved, and these difficult schedules have their own unique challenges. My husband and I have dealt with this intermittently throughout our married life. Yet when shift work isn't involved, most of us would do far better countering that drift if we slept together and woke up together.

For me, that has meant that I've had to make myself turn in earlier and get up earlier so I can share a cup of coffee with Keith before he goes to work. He needs to leave the house by 6:30 many days, and that's a big sacrifice for me, since I work at home and could sleep until 9:00 if I wanted to. Yet once you're used to it, it isn't that big a deal. And it starts the day right.

I wanted to end the book with this suggestion because it is such a relatively easy thing: turn in together. When you stop assuming that staying close is natural, and realize it's drifting that is natural, then you'll be more intentional about staying together. But being intentional doesn't always require huge changes. Sometimes just making little tweaks in how we do life can stop that drift.

A GOOD MARRIAGE ISN'T BY ACCIDENT

We've now looked at nine thoughts that, I trust, have challenged the way you look at marriage. It's not about sitting back and hoping someone else makes your relationship awesome. It's not about stuffing down your feelings or trying to keep peace. It's about throwing your energy and your efforts into achieving that oneness you desire. It's about being *intentional.*

It comes from seeing the wedding as the beginning—not the end—of the work you do to stay in love. It comes from deciding, every day, *I am going to love this man.* It comes from deciding to be good.

Good? That may sound strange, but perhaps that's the thought that best encompasses the other nine. A great marriage is not about being nice; a great marriage is about being *good.* And too many women focus on the nice—"I've got my happy face on today!"—and miss the good.

A nice woman wants to put others at ease, but she does this largely by dealing with surface issues and ignoring the important underlying heart issues. She isn't intentional; she reacts to what is going on around her. A good woman, on the other hand, acts. She wants to be part of what God is doing. And sometimes that ends up seeming not very nice.

It wasn't nice of Lily to stop paying the bills and to start putting consequences in place if her husband didn't fulfill his responsibilities, but it was good. It wasn't nice of Paul to call out Peter in public, but it was good. It isn't nice of a wife to say, "I find when we're making love that you're a little rough and it's difficult for me to enjoy it. Can we look at how to make my body feel more aroused too?" but it is good. It isn't nice of a mom to say to her children, "You need to sleep in your own beds without whining, because Daddy and I need to be together," but it is good. It doesn't sound nice to whisper to your husband, "Do you know what I want to do to you tonight?" while you also let your hands wander, but it is *very* good.

Being intentional about making our marriages strong the way God intended is being good—even when it is sometimes hard. As Jennifer Degler and Paul Coughlin pointed out in their book *No More Christian Nice Girl*, "Jesus says in Matthew 5:13, 'You are the salt of the earth,' not the sugar of the earth."[11] We're meant to preserve things so that they stay fresh; we're not just meant to make things sweeter to disguise what's rotten underneath.

Being intentional matters. But here's the good news: It's not just that being intentional is the right and moral thing to do. It's that being intentional—and putting these things into practice— also tends to give us that marriage we dream about.

In their awesome book *The Case for Marriage,* Linda Waite and Maggie Gallagher crunched the numbers from all the reliable marriage surveys they could find. One of the most interesting studies they quoted had to do with happiness and divorce. Several thousand couples were asked to rate their marriages on a scale from one to eight, with eight being lousy and one being marvel- ous. Then everyone who had rated their marriage a seven or eight was followed for five years.

The researchers discovered that the couples who divorced dur- ing those five years were more likely to report personal unhappiness at the five-year mark than the couples who had stayed together. Even more interestingly, 87 percent of the couples who stayed together now rated their marriages happier than they had previously, and 78 percent of those happier couples rated it the highest they could. They may have started out as the saddest, but they ended up the happiest.[12]

Just because you're in a rough patch, then, does not mean that you're destined to stay there. Sticking to your vows often improves your marriage virtually on its own. If you're going to stay in this marriage and shut that back door tight, then you likely decide that you had better make it work! You face what you're doing wrong and start asking God to change *you*. You decide to forgive and let some things slide. You fill your life with things that make you happy. You deal with the underlying issues. And slowly but surely, your marriage grows stronger.

When you walked down the aisle, you believed that this man was going to make you happy for the rest of your life. You've probably realized by now that he doesn't have that power. But if you're intentional—if you surrender yourself to what God wants to do in and through you, and if you start taking responsibility for the things in your control—you'll find that he is the person *with whom* you can be happy for the rest of your life. And that is a beautiful blessing indeed.

Summary of Action Steps

1. Figure out your husband's spiritual bent. Acknowledge it and validate it.

2. Make prayer a regular part of your marriage.

3. Share your "consolation" and "desolation" daily.

4. Brainstorm ways to spend time together "side by side" on a weekly basis.

5. Ask your husband, "Do I favor the kids over you?" Listen to what he says without commenting or getting defensive.

6. Set a bedtime for when you retire together.

Acknowledgments

Marriage is the most fun research project I've ever done—and Keith and I aren't finished yet! I'm eternally grateful for my husband. Honey, you're always saying I'm the more selfless one, but I know better. I'd do it all over again with you—even those first few years. So excited to see what the next few years of ministry has for us.

This book was really a labor of love—or at least a labor of some sort! I had health issues (totally non-life-threatening) galore, and yet I still met my deadlines. This was pretty much entirely due to my husband; my mom (who lets me bounce everything off her); my best friend, Susan Douglas; and my amazing kids, including Rebecca, who let me live in her townhouse for three weeks when I needed to escape and just write. Thank you all so much, and I hope our days of relying on takeout are behind us.

And in that labor, Ginger Kolbaba, my editor, was my doula. Ginger, there were times I really didn't like you. But now I'm your biggest fan! The process was hard, but I'm so happy with the final result.

Chip MacGregor, my agent, has been a great advocate and friend. Thanks for believing in me and for going to bat for me so enthusiastically.

Laura Barker and the team at WaterBrook championed this

book from the beginning. Thank you for your support and for welcoming me to Colorado Springs!

Shaunti Feldhahn, Gary Thomas, Leslie Vernick, Bill and Pam Farrel, and Shannon Ethridge are personal friends who have contributed so much to the marriage field. Thank you for letting me use your insights in this book. It is a privilege to partner with you.

To Holly Smith and Tammy Arseneau who work behind the scenes to keep *To Love, Honor and Vacuum,* my blog, and my speaking schedule going. It's wonderful to leave all of that in your capable hands when I have to write. And I love having friends to vent to when necessary as well! And to Barb Kenniphaas, who helped me with an early version of this book, I so appreciate your feedback and your dedication to proper comma usage.

To Sharol and Neil Josephson, Derek and Lisa Wood, and Mollie and Craig Sitwell. Thank you for your friendship and for your stories that made it here! We love you guys.

To my daughter Rebecca. I pictured you while I was writing this. So excited to be mother of the bride! Connor, thank you for entering our lives and becoming my son-in-love.

To my daughter Katie. I love our morning walks when I need to decompress. Perhaps I have shared more about marriage messes with you than I should have given your age, but at least you shall be well equipped in the future! I will miss you so much next year, but I'm looking forward to the next chapter in your life.

To my mother, Elizabeth Wray. You are the wisest person I know. I hope I have communicated some of that wisdom here.

Finally, to all my faithful readers at *To Love, Honor and Vac-*

uum. I am humbled that so many of you read what I write. I appreciate the comments, the e-mails, and, of course, the answers you all give in a hurry when I desperately need material and I post a question on Facebook. Many of you made it into this book, and it is richer because of you. With God's help, I hope to keep pointing you all to him and inspiring you to grow an even better marriage!

Discussion Questions

1. Sheila observed that it is often easier to show kindness to strangers than to those closest to us because we know our loved ones' dirty laundry. When do you have the hardest time being kind to your husband? Have you ever tried showing kindness deliberately, despite your feelings? What was the result?

2. One night your husband comes home late, and it doesn't bother you at all. Another night he's tardy, and your blood pressure boils. What makes the difference? What "trigger points" are most active in your marriage? How might being aware of your triggers help you respond differently?

3. We may know in our heads that "love is an action, not a feeling" and that "happiness is something you create, not something that happens." However, our culture sends a different message. What fairy tales do we hear about love and marriage? How do these fairy tales undermine our efforts to build a good marriage? What truths can we use to fight against the destructiveness of those fairy tales?

4. Quite often the solution to a marriage problem isn't for our husbands to change—it's for us to change. Sheila lists four

types of changes we can make: ask our husbands for specific help; include things in our lives that bring us joy, instead of waiting for our husbands to supply it; quit overfunctioning; and let others reap what they sow. Have you ever tried one of these approaches? How did it work? Which change, if any, do you feel God calling you to make now? What result do you anticipate?

5. What differing definitions of *submission* have you heard? How do they compare with the way Sheila explained it? How might our understanding of submission shape our marriages in good ways and bad?

6. When you were growing up, what model of conflict resolution did you most often witness: peacemaking or peacekeeping? How has your background influenced the way that you approach conflicts? Think of a recent conflict in your marriage; what would it look like for you to apply peacemaking in that situation?

7. Do you agree that conflict can be good for a marriage? Explain your answer. What are some healthy boundaries you've drawn to ensure you "fight fair"?

8. "Just do it." Women have been inundated with that message when it comes to sex. Men need it, God commands it, so get to it! Have you heard any version of that message? If so, what was your response? What is a healthier approach to

improving sex and intimacy within marriage? Do you think the "why" of making love matters in the long run?

9. Few couples find praying together easy. Add to this challenge our loaded ideas of what makes a spiritual leader, and couples often find themselves spiritually distant from each other. What ideas have you gleaned about how to grow closer together with God? How much of a priority is spiritual intimacy in your marriage? How could you give it more emphasis without making your husband uncomfortable?

10. What "currents" are causing you and your husband to drift apart? What practical solutions that Sheila mentions would stop that drift? What other steps could you take to stay close together?

11. The theme of this book is that the way we think about marriage will influence the way we act in our marriage. Which of the nine thoughts has been the most challenging for you? How will adopting a new thought pattern change a specific aspect of your marriage?

Appendix

The following marriage books and resources are my favorites in these categories:

Make Your Marriage Great!

Chapman, Gary. *The Five Love Languages: The Secret to Love That Lasts.* Chicago: Northfield, 2009.

Farrel, Bill and Pam Farrel. *Men Are Like Waffles, Women Are Like Spaghetti.* Sisters, OR: Harvest House, 2007.

Feldhahn, Shaunti. *The Surprising Secrets of Highly Happy Marriages: The Little Things That Make a Big Difference.* Colorado Springs: Multnomah, 2013.

Feldhahn, Shaunti with Tally Whitehead. *The Good News About Marriage: Debunking Discouraging Myths About Marriage and Divorce.* Colorado Springs: Multnomah, 2014.

Thomas, Gary. *A Lifelong Love: What If Marriage Is About More Than Just Staying Together?* Colorado Springs: David C. Cook, 2014.

The Purpose of Marriage

Keller, Timothy. *The Meaning of Marriage: Facing the Complexities of Commitment with the Wisdom of God.* New York: Riverhead Reprint, 2011.

Mason, Mike. *The Mystery of Marriage: Meditations on the Miracle.* Colorado Springs: Multnomah, 2012.

Thomas, Gary. *Sacred Marriage: What If God Designed Marriage to Make Us Holy More Than to Make Us Happy?* Grand Rapids: Zondervan, 2008.

Sex

DeMuth, Mary. *Not Marked: Finding Hope and Healing after Sexual Abuse.* Rockwall, TX: Uncaged Publishing, 2013.

Ethridge, Shannon. *The Passion Principles: Celebrating Sexual Freedom in Marriage.* Nashville: Thomas Nelson, 2014.

Gregoire, Sheila Wray. *The Good Girl's Guide to Great Sex: And You Thought Bad Girls Have All the Fun.* Grand Rapids: Zondervan, 2012.

Gregoire, Sheila Wray. *31 Days to Great Sex.* Winnipeg, MB: WordAlive, 2013.

McCluskey, Christopher and Rachel McCluskey. *When Two Become One: Enhancing Sexual Intimacy in Marriage.* Grand Rapids: Revell, 2006.

Tiede, Vicki. *When Your Husband Is Addicted to Pornography: Healing Your Wounded Heart.* Greensboro, NC: New Growth, 2012.

Wheat, Ed, MD and Gaye Wheat. *Intended for Pleasure: Sex Technique and Sexual Fulfillment in Christian Marriage.* Grand Rapids: Revell, 2010.

If pornography is a problem in your marriage, Covenant Eyes offers Internet accountability for your phones, computers,

and devices. http://covenanteyes.com. Use coupon code
TLHV to get one month free.

Handling Conflict and Setting Boundaries

Cloud, Dr. Henry and Dr. John Townsend. *Boundaries in Marriage: Understanding the Choices That Make or Break Loving Relationships.* Grand Rapids: Zondervan, 1999.

Dobson, James. *Love Must Be Tough: New Hope for Marriages in Crisis.* Wheaton: Tyndale, 2010.

Downs, Tim and Joy Downs. *Fight Fair: Winning at Conflict Without Losing at Love.* Chicago: Moody, 2010.

Townsend, John. *Who's Pushing Your Buttons? Handling the Difficult People in Your Life.* Nashville: Thomas Nelson, 2007.

Vernick, Leslie. *How to Act Right When Your Spouse Acts Wrong.* Colorado Springs: WaterBrook, 2011.

Vernick, Leslie. *The Emotionally Destructive Marriage: How to Find Your Voice and Reclaim Your Hope.* Colorado Springs: WaterBrook, 2013.

Roles in Marriage

Crabb, Dr. Larry. *Fully Alive: A Biblical Vision of Gender That Frees Men and Women to Live Beyond Stereotypes.* Grand Rapids: Baker, 2013.

Degler, Jennifer and Paul Coughlin. *No More Christian Nice Girl: When Just Being Nice — Instead of Good — Hurts You, Your Family, and Your Friends.* Minneapolis: Bethany House, 2010.

Gregoire, Sheila Wray. *To Love, Honor and Vacuum: When You Feel More Like a Maid Than a Wife and Mother* (second edition). Grand Rapids: Kregel, 2014.

Lewis, Robert and William Hendricks. *Rocking the Roles: Building a Win-Win Marriage.* Colorado Springs: Nav-Press, 1999.

Scazzero, Geri. *The Emotionally Healthy Woman: Eight Things You Have to Quit to Change Your Life.* Grand Rapids: Zondervan, 2013.

Notes

We Do What We Think!

1. Taken from 1 Peter 3:1. In the context of this verse, it's clear that Peter is talking about winning nonbelieving husbands to Christ. However, in many Christian circles this verse has been expanded to all aspects of marriage, insinuating that if a wife disagrees with what her husband does, she should sit back and be silent and thus encourage him to change because of her godliness.
2. Ephesians 6:10.

Thought #1: My Husband Is My Neighbor

1. See Matthew 19:4–6.
2. Larry Osborne, *Accidental Pharisees: Avoiding Pride, Exclusivity, and the Other Dangers of an Overzealous Faith* (Grand Rapids: Zondervan, 2012), 163–64.
3. Gary Thomas, "Father-in-Law," *Gary Thomas: Closer to Christ, Closer to Others,* October 29, 2014, www .garythomas.com/fatherinlaw/.
4. Bill Farrel and Pam Farrel, *Men Are Like Waffles, Women Are Like Spaghetti* (Sisters, OR: Harvest House, 2007).

Thought #2: My Husband Can't Make Me Mad

1. Peter Kreeft, *Prayer for Beginners* (San Francisco: Ignatius, 2000), Kindle edition, chapter 18, paragraph 4.

2. PinkPad is a popular cycle tracker where you can record your moods, your physical symptoms—even when you make love—so that you can chart your libido. It helps you figure out your fertile periods too. You can find it here: http://pinkp.ad/pinkpad/home.

3. See, for example, Emerson Eggerichs, *Love and Respect: The Love She Most Desires; The Respect He Desperately Needs* (Nashville: Thomas Nelson, 2004).

4. From the "Highly Happy Marriages" speech given by Shaunti Feldhahn, October 25, 2014, on behalf of Neeje Association for Women and Family, Ottawa, Ontario, Canada.

5. Shaunti Feldhahn, *The Surprising Secrets of Highly Happy Marriages* (Colorado Springs: Multnomah, 2013), 30.

6. Feldhahn, *Secrets of Highly Happy Marriages,* 221.

7. Personal story a reader told me and gave me permission to use.

8. Feldhahn, *Secrets of Highly Happy Marriages,* 48.

9. Feldhahn, *Secrets of Highly Happy Marriages,* 49.

10. Feldhahn, *Secrets of Highly Happy Marriages,* 111.

Thought #3: My Husband Was Not Put on This Earth to Make Me Happy

1. L. J. Smith, *Secret Vampire,* Night World, vol. 1 (London: Hodder Children's Books, 1997), 68.

2. Rainbow Rowell, *Eleanor & Park* (New York: St. Martin's Griffin, 2013), 301.

3. Gary Thomas, *The Sacred Search: What If It's Not About Who You Marry, But Why?* (Colorado Springs: David C. Cook, 2013), 64.

4. For more on this concept see Matthew 6:33.

5. Deirdre Bair, "The 40-Year Itch," *New York Times,* June 3, 2010, www.nytimes.com/2010/06/04/opinion/04bair.html?_r=0.

6. C. S. Lewis, *Surprised by Joy* (Glasgow, Scotland: Fount Paperback, 1955), 20.

7. Shaunti Feldhahn, *The Surprising Secrets of Highly Happy Marriages* (Colorado Springs: Multnomah, 2013), 178.

8. Feldhahn, *Secrets of Highly Happy Marriages,* 185.

Thought #4: I Can't Mold My Husband into My Image

1. Becky Zerbe, "The List That Saved My Marriage," *Today's Christian Woman,* September 2008, www.todayschristianwoman.com/articles/2008/september/list-that-saved-my-marriage.html.

2. Dr. Henry Cloud and Dr. John Townsend, *Boundaries in Marriage: Understanding the Choices That Make or Break Loving Relationships* (Grand Rapids: Zondervan, 1999), 18.

3. Ellie Lisitsa, "The Four Horsemen: Contempt," *The Gottman Relationship Blog,* May 15, 2013, www.gottmanblog.com/four-horsemen/2014/10/30/the-four-horsemen-contempt.

4. For more on Cheri Gregory's Complaint-Free Challenge, visit her website at www.cherigregory.com/the-purse-onality-challenge-31-days-of-replacing-baditude-with-gods-word-and-gratitude/.

5. Shaunti Feldhahn with Tally Whitehead, *The Good News About Marriage: Debunking Discouraging Myths About Marriage and Divorce* (Colorado Springs: Multnomah, 2014), 117.

6. Geri Scazzero, *The Emotionally Healthy Woman: Eight Things You Have to Quit to Change Your Life* (Grand Rapids: Zondervan, 2013), 141.

7. Scazzero, *Emotionally Healthy Woman,* 144.

8. John Townsend, *Who's Pushing Your Buttons? Handling the Difficult People in Your Life* (Nashville: Thomas Nelson, 2007), Kindle edition, location 1527–29.

Thought #5: I'm Not in Competition with My Husband

1. *The Princess Bride,* directed by Rob Reiner, Act III Communications, 1987.

2. Wayne Grudem has written extensively on the meaning of *kephale,* arguing that it does not mean "source" but instead connotes authority. Others, however, have countered his writings. I find the latter more persuasive; you can read the different sides of the debate here: Berkeley and Alvera Mickelsen, "What Does Kephale Mean in the New Testament?" in *Women, Authority, and the Bible* (Downers Grove, IL: Inter Varsity Press, 1986), 97–110, and in Wayne Grudem,

"The Meaning of Kephale ('Head'): a response to recent studies." *Trinity Journal* 11NS (1990), 3–72. You'll find a synopsis of the arguments here: www.doxa.ws/social/Women/head2.html. To me, one of the most persuasive arguments is that if *kephale* must connote authority, then 1 Corinthians 11:3 puts our doctrine of the Trinity in jeopardy.

3. See, for example, Debi Pearl, *Created to Be His Help Meet* (Pleasantville, TN: No Greater Joy Ministries, 2004), as one author who feels that women's primary identity is only found in relation to their "helping" their husbands.

4. Carolyn Custis James, "The Return of the Ezer," Whitby Forum, December 5, 2005, www.whitbyforum.com/2005/12/return-of-ezer.html.

5. Dr. Larry Crabb, *Fully Alive: A Biblical Vision of Gender That Frees Men and Women to Live Beyond Stereotypes* (Grand Rapids: Baker, 2013), 50.

6. Crabb, *Fully Alive,* 50.

7. See Gary Thomas, *Sacred Marriage: What If God Designed Marriage to Make Us Holy More Than to Make Us Happy?* (Grand Rapids: Zondervan, 2008), for an in-depth look at this concept.

8. Another example would be in 1 Corinthians 7 where couples are told how to value sex in marriage.

9. Jennifer Wilkin, "When Dad Doesn't Disciple the Kids," *The Beginning of Wisdom,* October 22, 2014, http://jenwilkin.blogspot.com/2014/10/when-dad-doesnt-disciple-kids.html.

Thought #6: I'm Called to Be a Peacemaker, Not a Peacekeeper

1. See Acts 10.

2. LiveScience Staff, "Spouses Who Fight Live Longer,"
   LiveScience, January 23, 2008, www.livescience.com/4814
   -spouses-fight-live-longer.html.

3. Quoted by Billy Graham at the funeral of his wife, Ruth,
   www.ruthbellgrahammemorial.org/rbg_memories.asp.

4. Nina Roesner, "Have You Morphed into His Mom by
   Doing It All? Respect Dare #33," *The Respect Dare,* downloaded from http://ninaroesner.com/2014/09/02/have-you
   -morphed-into-his-mom-by-doing-it-all-respect-dare-33
   /, December 14, 2014.

5. Robert Lewis and William Hendricks, *Rocking the Roles:
   Building a Win-Win Marriage* (Colorado Springs: Nav-
   Press, 1999), 183–86.

Thought #7: Being One Is More Important Than Being Right

1. Quoted at Smart Marriages Marriage Quotes, www
   .smartmarriages.com/marriage.quotes.html.

2. Gary Chapman, *The Five Love Languages: The Secret to
   Love That Lasts* (Chicago: Northfield, 2009).

Thought #8: Having Sex Is Not the Same as Making Love

1. Dominic Midgley, "Why Are We Having Less Sex?" *Daily
   Express,* November 27, 2013, www.express.co.uk/life-style
   /life/445342/Why-are-we-all-having-less-sex.

2. Sheila Wray Gregoire, *The Good Girl's Guide to Great Sex*
   (Grand Rapids: Zondervan, 2012), 247.

3. Gregoire, *Good Girl's Guide to Great Sex,* 249.

4. See, for example, where pastor Ed Young of The Fellowship Church in Grapevine, Texas, made headlines, even on CNN, by challenging his congregation to have sex every day for a week. Setrige Crawford, "Texas Pastor Challenges Congregation to Have More Sex," *The Christian Post,* January 9, 2012, www.christianpost.com/news/texas -pastor-challenges-congregation-to-have-more-sex-66738/.

5. Ron Gavrieli, "Why I Stopped Watching Porn," TED Talks, October 26, 2013, www.youtube.com/watch?v=gRJ _QfP2mhU. (TED stands for Technology, Entertainment, Design.)

6. Rachel B. Duke, "More Women Lured to Internet Pornog-raphy," *Washington Times,* July 11, 2010, www .washingtontimes.com/news/2010/jul/11/more -women-lured-to-pornography-addiction/?page=all.

7. "Scientists: Too Much Internet Porn May Cause Impo-tence," NewCore, *Fox News,* February 25, 2011, www.foxnews.com/health/2011/02/25/scientists -internet-porn-cause-impotence/.

8. Gregoire, *Good Girl's Guide to Great Sex,* 28.

9. Tyger Latham, "Does Porn Contribute to ED?" Therapy Matters, *Psychology Today,* May 3, 2012, www.psychology today.com/blog/therapy-matters/201205/does-porn -contribute-ed.

10. Carrie Armstrong, "ACOG Guideline on Sexual Dysfunc-tion in Women," *American Family Physician* 84, no. 6 (Sept. 15, 2011): 705–9.

11. Jennifer Smith, "Why I Chose to Get Rid of Parabens & What I Use Instead!" February 20, 2014, http://unveiled wife.com/why-i-chose-to-get-rid-of-parabens-what-i-use -instead/.

12. Gregoire, *Good Girl's Guide to Great Sex,* 246.

13. See Rajdeep's whole story at "Honeymoon Blues to 'O'ver the Rainbow," *To Love, Honor and Vacuum,* October 9, 2012, http://tolovehonorandvacuum.com/2012/10 /honeymoon-blues-to-over-the-rainbow/.

14. Mary DeMuth, "Wifey Wednesday: Sexual Abuse Really Messes with Your Sex Life," *To Love, Honor and Vacuum,* April 16, 2014, http://tolovehonorandvacuum.com/2014/04 /sexual-abuse-messes-with-sex-life/.

Thought #9: If I'm Not Careful, We'll Drift Apart

1. Shaunti Feldhahn, *The Good News About Marriage* (Colorado Springs: Multnomah, 2014), 75.

2. Blaise Pascal, *Pensées,* 1670.

3. Shaunti Feldhahn, *The Surprising Secrets of Highly Happy Marriages* (Colorado Springs: Multnomah, 2013), 189.

4. Gary Thomas, *Sacred Pathways: Discover Your Soul's Path to God* (Grand Rapids: Zondervan, 2010).

5. John and Stasi Eldredge, *Love & War: Find Your Way to Something Beautiful in Your Marriage* (Colorado Springs: WaterBrook, 2011), 127.

6. Feldhahn, *Secrets of Highly Happy Marriages,* 147.

7. Feldhahn, *Secrets of Highly Happy Marriages,* 145.

8. From the book *Sleeping with Bread: Holding What Gives You Life* by Dennis Linn, Sheila Fabricant Linn, and Matthew Linn (Mahwah, NJ: Paulist Press, 1995).

9. From a personal conversation, May 28, 2014.

10. A multitude of studies exist showing the benefits of children growing up in a married, two-parent family. Here, for example, is a report of one such study: W. Bradford Wilcox, "Marriage Makes Our Children Richer—Here's Why," *The Atlantic,* October 29, 2013, www.theatlantic.com/business /archive/2013/10/marriage-makes-our-children-richer-heres -why/280930/. Another study, specifically on obesity and divorce, can be found here: Cari Nierenberg, "Children of Divorce May Be More Likely to Be Overweight," *LiveScience,* June 5, 2014, www.foxnews.com/science /2014/06/04/children-divorce-may-be-more-likely-to -be-overweight/.

11. Jennifer Degler and Paul Coughlin, *No More Christian Nice Girl: When Just Being Nice—Instead of Good—Hurts You, Your Family and Your Friends* (Minneapolis: Bethany House, 2010), Kindle edition, location 403–18.

12. Linda J. Waite and Maggie Gallagher, *The Case for Marriage: Why Married People Are Happier, Healthier, and Better Off Financially* (New York: Random House, 2002).